THE INSIDER'S GUIDE

Criminal Justice Resources on the Internet

2002

Ken Strutin

New York State Defenders Association

Copyright © 2002 New York State Defenders Association
194 Washington Avenue, Suite 500
Albany, NY 12210
(518) 465-3524

ISBN 0-9718982-0-0

All rights reserved. Printed in the United States of America.

Nothing contained in this book is to be considered as the rendering of legal advice for specific cases, and readers are responsible for obtaining advice from their own legal counsel. This book and any forms and agreements herein are intended for educational and informational purposes only and are not a substitute for the advice of an attorney. If you require legal or other expert advice, you should seek the services of a competent attorney or other professional.

The products and services mentioned in this publication are under or may be under trademark or service mark protection. Product and service names and terms are used throughout only in an editorial fashion, to the benefit of the product manufacturer or service provider, with no intention of infringement. Use of a product or service name or term in this publication should not be regarded as affecting the validity of any trademark or service mark.

Please note that inclusion of web sites in this book is not an endorsement or approval of any commercial advertising, products, services or opinions of those web sites. The web sites provided here are for informational purposes only. NYSDA does not bear any responsibility for the accuracy, validity or the content of any of the web sites. If there are problems with a particular web site, contact that site's webmaster.

Discounts are available for books ordered in bulk. Special consideration may be given to bar associations, CLE programs, bar-related organizations, public defenders, assigned counsel, and legal aid attorneys. Inquire at the address above.

CONTENTS

Acknowledgements i
About the Author ii
Feedback ii
Foreword iii
Preface iv
Abbreviations vi

PART I

NEW INTERNET RESOURCES 1

PART II

INTERNET RESOURCES COLLECTION 107

Glossary 171
Further Reading 173
Companion CD-ROM 174

ACKNOWLEDGEMENTS

I wish to thank the entire staff at the New York State Defenders Association (NYSDA) for their support, encouragement, ideas and suggestions. I commend their daily efforts on behalf of those most in need, and thank them for sharing their wisdom and experience. Like all projects, this one builds on earlier work, including the development of the "Resources Sighted, Cited and Sited" section of the *Public Defense Backup Center REPORT,* now found on the NYSDA web site, www.nysda.org.

I would like to acknowledge specifically those people who played a prominent role in the evolution and production of *The Insider's Guide.* The NYSDA web site, which was the first showcase for the raw materials culled for this book, owes much of its vitality to the efforts of Dave Austin, Web Master and Director of Information Technology at the Backup Center. The work and insights of Shahrul Ladue, NYSDA's Legal Secretary, greatly facilitated the planning and production of this book. I also thank Larry O'Brien for his assistance and helpful comments regarding design and format.

The Insider's Guide and NYSDA's web site would not have come into existence without the guidance, editorial efforts, and thoughtful suggestions of Charles F. O'Brien, NYSDA's Managing Attorney. Finally, this book and NYSDA's other accomplishments over the past twenty years are attributable to the support of NYSDA's Executive Director, Jonathan E. Gradess.

ABOUT THE AUTHOR

Ken Strutin (J.D., M.L.S.) is a legal information consultant, experienced criminal defense attorney and well-known writer and speaker. He has lectured extensively about the benefits of using the Internet for legal research at national and local CLE training programs for criminal defense lawyers, capital defenders and legal aid attorneys. He is the author of *ALI-ABA's Practice Checklist Manual on Representing Criminal Defendants* and co-author of the award winning *Legal Research Methodology* computer tutorial, published by the Center for Computer-Assisted Legal Instruction (CALI). He has contributed chapters to several books and written many articles concerning knowledge management, legal research and criminal law. Mr. Strutin has taught courses in *Advanced Legal Research* and *Law Office Management*. He is listed in *Who's Who in American Law* and is a member of *Beta Phi Mu*, the International Library Honor Society. Currently, Mr. Strutin does consulting work for the New York State Defenders Association.

FEEDBACK

The New York State Defenders Association is committed to serving our readers' needs; we welcome your feedback on how we can improve future editions of this book. If you have a comment about *The Insider's Guide* or a new resource to share, please contact Ken Strutin.

New York State Defenders Association
194 Washington Avenue, Suite 500
Albany, NY 12210
(518) 465-3524
kstrutin@nysda.org

FOREWORD

The Internet can be as frustrating as it is amazing. Hours can be wasted wading through useless web links before finding what you're interested in. After crafting what you think is a carefully defined search query on your favorite search engine, it is easy to become disheartened with the 10,000 "relevant" hits that are returned. Or after spending days or weeks searching the web for a particular topic, you finally stumble across a great resource that has evaded you. The Internet is vast and today's search engines can only explore and index a fraction of it. While new search tools are being developed to tap hidden resources in the "invisible web," the simple fact is that there are great portions of the web that elude search engines and web crawlers.

Valuable, free online resources - case law, statutes, forensic studies, reports, briefs, motions, investigative tools, and an extensive library of research materials - are of little use if they can't be easily located. NYSDA's goal in publishing the *Insider's Guide* is to provide researchers and busy practitioners with a current compilation of significant criminal justice and public defense resources on the Internet. Ken Strutin has spent hundreds of hours locating recently published or updated criminal justice and defense resources on the web. This *Guide* and the accompanying CD-ROM are the result of those many hours. They will assist even experienced Internet users in quickly locating valuable and frequently hard to find resources, saving time and hopefully minimizing frustration.

Charles F. O'Brien
Managing Attorney
New York State Defenders Association

PREFACE

The Insider's Guide is the culmination of more than two years of work reviewing and evaluating thousands of web-based criminal justice resources, publications and products. It contains the most relevant and current resources organized by subject area. Not every web site or publication on a topic is listed, and while most publications are recent, selected older publications have been included because of their importance. Articles or press releases summarizing a lengthy report or complex web site have been included to save the time of the user.

The Insider's Guide is organized in two parts. Part I highlights and describes new publications and web sites appearing in the past few years. Part II is a comprehensive collection of web resources, encompassing some of the newer sites and previously existing ones. *The Insider's Guide* complements the national and local news and resources routinely published on the New York State Defenders Association (NYSDA) web site, www.nysda.org.

The New York State Defenders Association is a not-for-profit membership organization that has been providing support to New York's criminal defense community since 1967. Its mission is to improve the quality and scope of publicly supported legal representation to low-income people. In 1995, NYSDA established one of the first criminal defense sites on the Internet. Since then, the web site has expanded to meet the growing information needs of the public defense community in New York and elsewhere. It contains many of the research links appearing in *The Insider's Guide* and thousands more concerning current news items, court decisions, motions and research studies.

The intent behind *The Insider's Guide* was to create a reference source for researchers and practitioners. Thus, the layout has been designed to make it convenient for browsing in print and accessing the web sites through the CD-ROM. The full web addresses have been included for each site for technical reasons, such as enabling readers to deal with web sites that have become problematic. For example, a link may not work because a web site is down for repair, updating or retooling. It may have some other quirk that requires the web address to be cut and pasted into the web browser's address bar to function. Hopefully, you will not encounter too many difficulties in trying to reach the web sites in this book.

The focus of *The Insider's Guide* is on web sites, publications and products. It does not address Internet usage, such as transferring files, joining listservs or managing email. An effort has been made to present broad-based resources useful to practitioners and researchers nationally. Due to NYSDA's New York orientation, there are a significant number of New York resources listed. No attempt has been made to cull all resources from all states, though many not listed here might exist.

All of the web addresses in *The Insider's Guide* were active as of the date of publication. In Part II a dollar sign ($) has been added to web sites to indicate that there may be a fee associated with using it, such as a commercial database. Like any characteristic of a web site, the free or fee status may change over time. A companion CD-ROM containing the full text and active links to all the web addresses has been included. Any link appearing in the *Guide* can be accessed directly through the CD-ROM. Details about the CD-ROM appear at the end of this book.

Ken Strutin
Legal Information Consultant

ABBREVIATIONS

ABA	American Bar Association
ABCNY	Association of the Bar of the City of New York
ACCD	American Council of Chief Defenders (NLADA)
ACLU	American Civil Liberties Union
AI	Amnesty International
ALI	American Law Institute
ALSO	American Law Sources Online
AO	Administrative Office of the U.S. Courts
APRL	Association of Professional Responsibility Lawyers
BJA	U.S. Bureau of Justice Assistance
BJS	U.S. Bureau of Justice Statistics
BOP	Federal Bureau of Prisons
CANY	Correctional Association of New York
CASA	National Center on Addiction and Substance Abuse at Columbia University
CCI	Center for Court Innovation
CJRI	Criminal and Justice Research Institute
DOJ	U.S. Department of Justice
DOS	U.S. Department of State
DPIC	Death Penalty Information Center
FJC	U.S. Federal Judicial Center
GAO	U.S. Government Accounting Office
GPO	U.S. Government Printing Office
HRW	Human Rights Watch

LII	Legal Information Institute at Cornell University School of Law
LLRX	Law Library Resource Exchange
LOC	U.S. Library of Congress
LWVNY	League of Women Voters of New York State
NACDL	National Association of Criminal Defense Lawyers
NARA	National Archives and Records Administration
NHTSA	National Highway Traffic Safety Administration
NIJ	U.S. National Institute of Justice
NITA	National Institute of Trial Advocacy
NJC	National Judicial College
NLADA	National Legal Aid and Defender Association
NYCDO	N.Y. Capital Defender Office
NYCLA	New York County Lawyers' Association
NYCLU	N.Y. Civil Liberties Union
NYLJ	N.Y. Law Journal
NYSBA	N.Y. State Bar Association
NYT	New York Times
OCA	N.Y. Office of Court Administration
OJJDP	U.S. Office of Juvenile Justice and Delinquency Prevention
OJP	U.S. Office of Justice Programs
OVC	U.S. Office of Victim Services
USDC	U.S. District Court
USSC	U.S. Sentencing Commission
VIJ	Vera Institute of Justice

PART I

NEW INTERNET RESOURCES

CONTENTS

APPELLATE PRACTICE	5
ASSIGNED COUNSEL RATES	6
COURTS AND COURT DOCKETS	9
CRIMINAL HISTORIES	10
CRIMINAL JUSTICE	11
CRIMINAL JUSTICE STATISTICS	17
DEATH PENALTY	19
DNA	25
DRUG COURTS	27
DRUG LAWS	29
DWI	32
EXPERTS	33
EYEWITNESS EVIDENCE	33
FEDERAL COURTS	34
FEDERAL PRACTICE	35
FEDERAL SENTENCING	36
FORENSICS	36
FORMS	40
IMMIGRATION	41
INTERPRETERS	41
INVESTIGATIVE TOOLS	42
JURY INSTRUCTIONS	42
JUVENILE JUSTICE	43
LAW OFFICE MANAGEMENT	49
LAW OFFICE TECHNOLOGY	51
LEGAL RESEARCH	57
LEGAL SERVICES	62
LITIGATION	64
LOCATING INMATES	66
LOCATING LAWYERS	67
LOCATING PUBLIC OFFICIALS	68

MEDICAL INFORMATION	69
MENTAL ILLNESS	70
NEW YORK COURTS	71
POLICE MISCONDUCT	74
POST-CONVICTION	76
PRISON STATISTICS	77
PRISONERS' RIGHTS	79
PRISONS	83
PROBLEM SOLVING COURTS	84
PROFESSIONAL RESPONSIBILITY	85
PUBLIC DEFENSE	86
PUBLIC RECORDS	93
RACE AND LAW	94
REFERENCE TOOLS	96
RESEARCH TOOLS	99
SEARCH ENGINES	101
STATISTICS	103
TERRORISM LAW	103
WEB TOOLS	104
WRONGFUL CONVICTION	105

APPELLATE PRACTICE

ABC's of Appellate Law: A Guided Tour for Non-Specialists (Law.com) was a presentation of Law.com Seminars, at which appellate lawyers and justices of the California Court of Appeals discussed various practical issues in appellate practice.

- ABC's of Appellate Law: A Guided Tour for Non-Specialists
  www.law.com/cgi-bin/gx.cgi/AppLogic+FT
  ContentServer?pagename=law/View&c=Article&cid=ZZZYQAUVOJC&live=true&cst=1&pc=0&pa=0&s=News&ExpIgnore=true&showsummary=0

Briefsmart is an online brief bank and document exchange service. Motions and briefs on various subjects, including criminal law, can be located using their free search engine. The purchase costs of each document are indicated.

- Briefsmart
  www.briefsmart.com/

Federal Criminal Appeals, 1999 (BJS 2001). This report "[d]escribes the increase in the appellate caseload as a result of challenges to the sentence imposed. Following implementation of the Federal Sentencing Reform Act, which opened the sentencing process to appellate review, the number of criminal appeals filed doubled."

- Federal Criminal Appeals, 1999
  www.ojp.usdoj.gov/bjs/abstract/fca99.htm

Putting the Right (Type) Face on Your Appeal, Connecticut Law Tribune, November 12, 2001 discusses the efficacy of using the appropriate typeface for preparing an appellate brief.

- Putting the Right (Type) Face on Your Appeal
  www.law.com/cgi-bin/gx.cgi/AppLogic+FT
  ContentServer?pagename=law/View&c=Article&cid=ZZZ9BJ1URTC&live=true&cst=6&pc=0&pa=

0&s=News&ExpIgnore=
true&showsummary=0

Things Your Mentor Never Taught You About Briefs, New Jersey Law Journal, October 18, 2001 discusses pragmatic strategies for effective appellate brief writing.

- Things Your Mentor Never Taught You About Briefs www.law.com/cgi-bin/gx.cgi/AppLogic+FTContentServer?pagename=law/View&c=Article&cid=ZZZV6WFOXSC&live=true&cst=1&pc=0&pa=0&s=News&ExpIgnore=true&showsummary=0

ASSIGNED COUNSEL RATES

Assigned Counsel Compensation in New York: A Growing Crisis (OCA 2000). "This Report outlines the historical role of assigned counsel in New York, and it describes the dramatic impact that the exodus of attorneys from the assigned counsel panels has had on the justice system. The Report also discusses the Judiciary's recent efforts to convene representatives of the bar, law enforcement and local government to devise a solution to this problem. The Report describes the results of these efforts, sets forth a proposal to increase the current rates and identifies a source of funds to pay for the increase."

- Assigned Counsel Compensation in New York: A Growing Crisis www.courts.state.ny.us/18b.html

Committee to Promote Public Trust and Confidence in the Legal System (OCA 1999). "Increase funding for public defenders' offices. These offices handle not only criminal, but also Family Court and Surrogate's Court matters (County Law §§ 18-A and B). Attorneys in many public defenders' offices carry an excessive caseload which can compromise the quality of legal service that is rendered. Sufficient funds for investigators also are needed. Funding should be more proportionate to that given to District Attorneys' offices." "Increase compensation for assigned—appointed counsel under Judiciary Law § 35. The present fee structure of $25 per hour for out-of-court time and $40 per hour for in-court time was last amended in 1985 [sic]. This is wholly inadequate. As a result, capable, experienced attorneys are declining to serve as appointed or assigned counsel because they cannot afford to work at these rates and meet overhead expenses."

- Committee to Promote Public Trust and Confidence in the Legal System
www.courts.state.ny.us/pubtrust.pdf

Crisis in the Legal Representation of the Poor (Appellate Division First Department Committee on the Representation of the Poor 2001). The Committee completed an investigation into the state of "governmentally-funded legal representation of those who cannot afford counsel" in New York City and issued a report calling for increased funding for assigned counsel and additional funding and services for public defense.

- Crisis in the Legal Representation of the Poor
www.courts.state.ny.us/1AD-rep-poor.htm

Hourly Fees Paid By Various Federal Agencies to Private Attorneys for Legal Services (GAO 2001). This report contains information on hourly fees paid by the federal government to private attorneys for legal services from 1999 to 2001.

- Hourly Fees Paid By Various Federal Agencies to Private Attorneys for Legal Services
www.gao.gov/new.items/d01887r.pdf

Justice Denied: The Crisis in Legal Representation of Birth Parents in Child Protective Pro-

ceedings (NYC Public Advocate 2000). Child Planning and Advocacy Now, part of the Public Advocate's Office, issued a report critical of problems with the administration of court assigned attorneys handling family court matters in New York City.

- Justice Denied: The Crisis in Legal Representation of Birth Parents in Child Protective Proceedings pubadvocate.nyc.gov/documents/18bweb.PDF

Resolving the Assigned Counsel Fee Crisis: An Opportunity to Provide County Fiscal Relief and Quality Public Defense Services (NYSDA 2001) reviews defense systems in New York and other states, national studies and standards, and draws upon the collective experience of public defense service providers. It calls for the immediate increase of assigned counsel rates and the efficient and effective provision of public defense services.

- Resolving the Assigned Counsel Fee Crisis: An Opportunity to Provide County Fiscal Relief and Quality Public Defense Services www.nysda.org/ResolvingtheAssignedCounselFeeCrisis_01.pdf

State of the Judiciary Report (OCA 2001) "The situation has worsened. Assigned counsel fees . . . were barely adequate 15 years ago when they were set by the Legislature. Today, they have decimated assigned counsel panels. And the consequences are severe." The proposal to increase rates "$75 an hour for felony and Family Court cases, and $60 an hour for nonfelony cases" would be funded by expanding the collection of surcharges and fines. "It is the responsibility of all of us in government to address this deepening crisis now. We simply cannot let another year pass without resolving this problem."

- State of the Judiciary Report

www.courts.state.ny.us/
NYStateofJudiciary2001.
pdf

COURTS AND COURT DOCKETS

Court Rules, Forms and Dockets (LLRX) is a resource that contains over 700 links to federal and state courts. Published by the Law Library Resource Exchange, this resource has a powerful search tool and presents information in a well-organized fashion.

- Court Rules, Forms and Dockets
  www.llrx.com/courtrules
- Law Library Resource Exchange
  www.llrx.com

Keeping Up With Electronic Docket and Document Retrieval, Legal Dockets Online, October 22, 2001 is a thorough review and comparison of federal and state court records available online. It also includes discussions of official and commercial docket services.

- Keeping Up With Electronic Docket and Document Retrieval
  www.legaldockets.com/art1001.html

Legal Dockets Online provides free and inexpensive federal and state court case docket information. They maintain listings for all web accessible courts. They also maintain listings for accessing Federal and State opinions and news stories.

- Legal Dockets Online
  www.legaldockets.com/

Misdemeanor Courts, Hope for Crime Weary America (NJC 2000) is a report on the efficacy of volunteer citizen probation programs in misdemeanor courts in reducing recidivism and improving the response of the criminal justice system to defendants and victims.

- Misdemeanor Courts, Hope for Crime Weary America
  www.olemiss.edu/depts/mjc/Misdemeanor.pdf

Responding to the Community: Principles for Planning and Creating a Community Court (BJA 2001). "This bulletin is a guide for community justice planners, particularly those interested in court reform. Using the Midtown Community Court in New York City as a case study, the bulletin presents a set of common principles for community courts."

- Responding to the Community: Principles for Planning and Creating a Community Court www.ncjrs.org/pdffiles1/bja/185986.pdf

Videoconferencing Offers Solutions to Those Willing to Try, American Lawyer Media, October 22, 2001 is an article discussing the recent use of videoconferencing by the Nassau County Supreme Court in New York to reduce calendar call congestion in civil cases.

- Videoconferencing Offers Solutions to Those Willing to Try www.law.com/cgi-bin/gx.cgi/AppLogic+FTContentServer?pagename=law/View&c=Article&cid=ZZZH8DFFWSC&live=true&cst=6&pc=0&pa=0&s=News&ExpIgnore=true&showsummary=0

CRIMINAL HISTORIES

Navigating the Maze of Criminal Records Retrieval—Updated (LLRX June 1, 2001) is an article by Lynn Peterson, President of PFC Information Services, Inc., a public records research firm located in Oakland, California, that discusses methods for finding criminal histories nationwide using electronic databases.

- Navigating the Maze of Criminal Records Retrieval – Updated www.llrx.com/features/criminal2.htm

Public Attitudes Toward Uses of Criminal History Information (BJS 2001). "Presents the results of the first national survey of public attitudes towards use of criminal history information for a variety of purposes."

- Public Attitudes Toward Uses of Criminal History Information
www.ojp.usdoj.gov/bjs/abstract/pauchi.htm

Rapsheets.com is a subscription service that can access a database of more than 20 million records. The data is drawn from public records of state, county and local government agencies from around the nation.

- Rapsheets.com
www.rapsheets.com/

Report of the National Task Force on Privacy, Technology, and Criminal Justice Information (BJS 2001). "The task force reviewed the law and policy addressing the collection, use, and dissemination of criminal justice record information and, particularly, criminal history record information. The findings address a wide variety of issues which impact on privacy decisions and are relevant to persons considering the privacy impacts presented by advances in technology."

- Report of the National Task Force on Privacy, Technology, and Criminal Justice Information
www.ojp.usdoj.gov/bjs/abstract/rntfptcj.htm

Use and Management of Criminal History Record Information (BJS 2001). This report contains a comprehensive description of all aspects of the Federal and State criminal history record information systems.

- Use and Management of Criminal History Record Information
www.ojp.usdoj.gov/bjs/abstract/umchri01.htm

CRIMINAL JUSTICE 2000 Wiretap Report (AO 2001) was published by the Administrative Office of the United States Courts and provides information about wiretap and interception activities conducted by the federal government.

- 2000 Wiretap Report
  www.uscourts.gov/wiretap00/contents.html

Annual Report to Congress: Creating A Safer America: Fiscal Year 2000 (BJA 2001). "This Annual Report describes the funding and technical assistance BJA provided to state and local criminal justice systems in FY 2000."

- Annual Report to Congress: Creating A Safer America: Fiscal Year 2000
  www.ncjrs.org/pdffiles1/bja/187302.pdf

Crime and the Courts Channel (USLaw.com). It contains articles, resources and discussions about constitutional and criminal law. It also features a bulletin board where visitors can post questions.

- Crime and the Courts Channel
  www.uslaw.com/channel.tcl?channel_id=46

Criminal Justice 2000 (NIJ 2000). The National Institute of Justice asked dozens of experts to analyze current and emerging trends in criminal justice. Their analysis has been compiled into this four-volume series.

- Criminal Justice 2000
  www.ojp.usdoj.gov/nij/pubs-sum/cj2000.htm

Criminal Victimization 2000: Changes 1999-2000 With Trends 1993-2000 (BJS 2001). "According to the National Crime Victimization Survey, the violent crime rate fell 15% and the property crime rate fell 10%, 1999-2000. Overall property crime rates fell between 1999 and 2000 due to a decrease in theft and a slight decline in motor vehicle theft. From 1999 to 2000 violent crime rates fell for almost every demographic group considered: males, females, whites, blacks, non-Hispanics, and 12-to-24 year-olds."

- Criminal Victimization 2000: Changes 1999-

2000 With Trends 1993-2000
www.ojp.usdoj.gov/bjs/abstract/cv00.htm

Expenditure and Employment Statistics (BJS 2001) is a summary of statistics on the amounts of money that federal, state and local governments spend on criminal justice functions and personnel.

- Expenditure and Employment Statistics www.ojp.usdoj.gov/bjs/eande.htm

Facts About Cops: A Performance Overview of the Community Oriented Policing Services Program (Heritage Foundation 2000) is an evaluation of President Clinton's COPS program intended to place 100,000 more police officers on the streets to reduce crime.

- Facts About Cops: A Performance Overview of the Community Oriented Policing Services Program www.heritage.org/library/cda/cda00-10.html

Federal Criminal Case Processing, 2000: With Trends 1982-2000 (BJS 2001). "This report includes the number and disposition of suspects investigated by U.S. attorneys, the number of arrests for Federal offenses, the number of defendants in cases filed in U.S. district courts, the disposition of defendants in cases terminated in U.S. district courts, sanctions imposed on convicted defendants, the number of persons under Federal correctional supervision (probation, parole, supervised release, and incarceration), and trends in annual Federal criminal case processing."

- Federal Criminal Case Processing, 2000: With Trends 1982-2000 www.ojp.usdoj.gov/bjs/abstract/fccp00.htm

Felony Sentences in State Courts, 1998 (BJS 2001). This report examines the statistics for adults who were convicted of felonies and sentenced in state courts.

- Felony Sentences in State Courts, 1998
www.ojp.usdoj.gov/bjs/abstract/fssc98.htm

Firearm Use by Offenders (BJS 2001) describes firearm use by state and federal prison inmates during their current offense. Topics include types of firearms used, characteristics of inmates using firearms, why and where inmates used their firearms, and where they obtained their firearms.

- Firearm Use by Offenders
www.ojp.usdoj.gov/bjs/abstract/fuo.htm

Independent Technical Review of the Carnivore System: Final Report (DOJ 2000). This report evaluated Carnivore, a tool developed by the Federal Bureau of Investigation (FBI) to intercept electronic communications

- Independent Technical Review of the Carnivore System: Final Report
www.usdoj.gov/jmd/publications/carniv_final.pdf

Information Collection for Automated Mapping (Chicago Police Department 2000) is an electronic police blotter that allows residents of Chicago to learn about reported criminal activity in their area. Chicago Lets Citizens Map Crime, Federal Computer Week, October 5, 2000

- Information Collection for Automated Mapping
www.cityofchicago.org/caps/
- Chicago Lets Citizens Map Crime
www.fcw.com/civic/articles/2000/1002/web-chicago-10-05-00.asp

Multiple Homicide Cases Nationwide (NYT 2000). The New York Times created a research tool for studying multiple homicide cases across the country. A View of Rampage Killers Across the

Insider's Guide to Criminal Justice Resources

Country, New York Times, April 10, 2000 and The Well-Marked Roads to Homicidal Rage, New York Times, April 9, 2000.

- Multiple Homicide Cases Nationwide
www.nytimes.com/library/national/040900shoot-map.html
- A View of Rampage Killers Across the Country
www.nytimes.com/library/national/040900shoot-map.html
- The Well-Marked Roads to Homicidal Rage
www.nytimes.com/library/national/041000rampage-killers.html

NYSBA Special Committee on Administrative Adjudication Report (NYSBA 1999) is a study of the conditions and issues relating to administrative hearings conducted by various New York agencies, such as the Department of Motor Vehicles. Read about the report in Year Long Investigation of State Agencies Finds Motorists Don't Get a Fair Hearing at DMV, NYSBA Press Release, December 21, 1999.

- NYSBA Special Committee on Administrative Adjudication Report
www.nysba.org/whatsnew/report2.pdf
- Year Long Investigation of State Agencies Finds Motorists Don't Get a Fair Hearing at DMV
www.nysba.org/media/newsreleases/1999/admin.html

Research on Women and Girls in the Justice System (NIJ 2000) is a collection of conference studies that revealed a link between the victimization of women and their criminal behavior.

- Research on Women and Girls in the Justice System
www.ncjrs.org/pdffiles1/nij/180973.pdf

Small Area Income and Poverty Estimates: Intercensal Estimates for States, Counties, and

School Districts (U.S. Census 2001). "The main objective of this program is to provide updated estimates of income and poverty statistics for the administration of federal programs and the allocation of federal funds to local jurisdictions."

- Small Area Income and Poverty Estimates: Intercensal Estimates for States, Counties, and School Districts
www.census.gov/hhes/www/saipe.html

Social Science Research Network (Social Science Electronic Publishing) is a research library and network. It has an Abstract Database containing over 35,500 entries and an Electronic Paper Collection with over 18,100 downloadable full text documents.

- Social Science Research Network
www.ssrn.com/

State Court Prosecutors in Large Districts, 2001 (BJS 2001). "Presents data from the 2001 National Survey of Prosecutors. The report summarizes the budgets for prosecutors' offices that serve large districts and profiles their staffs of attorneys, investigators, victim advocates and support personnel. The other survey areas include the number of felony cases closed, the use of DNA evidence, and the number of juvenile cases proceeded against in criminal court."

- State Court Prosecutors in Large Districts, 2001
www.ojp.usdoj.gov/bjs/abstract/scpld01.htm

State Court Sentencing of Convicted Felons, 1998 (BJS 2001). This report examines data collected from a 1998 survey of felons convicted in state courts in over 300 counties.

- State Court Sentencing of Convicted Felons, 1998
www.ojp.usdoj.gov/bjs/abstract/scsc98st.htm

State of Criminal Justice (ABA Criminal Justice Section 2000). The sixth "State of Criminal Justice" report is a critical survey highlighting the directions in which the justice system is heading. It covers a wide range of topics from the death penalty to racial bias.

- State of Criminal Justice
  www.abanet.org/media/dec00/abareport.html

Summary of State and Local Justice Improvement Activities 2001 (ABA Committee on State Justice Initiatives 2001). "The Summary shows more than 1,000 areas of activity, including 331 'justice initiatives' that involve the public as well as the courts and bar associations."

- Summary of State and Local Justice Improvement Activities 2001
  www.abanet.org/justice/01summary/home.html

Vera Institute of Justice (VIJ) has revamped its web site providing a slick, user-friendly environment and access to its criminal justice publications, news and unique resources.

- Vera Institute of Justice
  www.vera.org/about/about_1.asp

Virtual Information Center (BJA 2001) The Bureau of Justice Assistance created a web search engine to locate information about innovative strategies and programs funded by the federal government.

- Virtual Information Center
  bjavic.aspensys.com/

CRIMINAL JUSTICE STATISTICS

Crime and Justice Data Online (BJS) is a web site for researchers who want to analyze statistics based on data from FBI Crime Reports and other government sources.

- Crime and Justice Data Online
  149.101.22.40/dataonline/

Crime Stats Made Easy Online, NYLJ, October 10, 2000 describes the many web resources available for finding criminal justice statistics.

- Crime Stats Made Easy Online
  www6.law.com/ny/tech/101000t5.html

Justice Research and Statistics Association web site is operated by a national nonprofit organization that conducts multistate research on statewide and system-wide problems such as domestic violence and convenience store crime, and practices such as community policing.

- Justice Research and Statistics Association
  www.jrsa.org/index.html

JUSTSTATS (BJS 2001) is a new listserv sponsored by the U.S. Department of Justice, Bureau of Justice Statistics. This free service routinely sends out notifications of new reports and links to full-text documents published by BJS and other agencies. Visit the Indigent Defense Statistics home page to see the kinds of reports available through this service.

- JUSTSTATS
  www.ojp.usdoj.gov/bjs/juststats.htm
- Indigent Defense Statistics
  www.ojp.usdoj.gov/bjs/id.htm

Sourcebook of Criminal Justice Statistics, 2000 (BJS 2001). This is a comprehensive compendium of criminal justice data covering such topics as: public attitudes toward crime and other criminal justice issues; nature and distribution of known offenses; characteristics and distribution of persons arrested; judicial processing of defendants; and persons under correctional supervision. The book is accessible online in a searchable format and individual sections can be downloaded.

- Sourcebook of Criminal Justice Statistics, 2000

www.ojp.usdoj.gov/bjs/abstract/scjsoo.htm
- Sourcebook of Criminal Justice Statistics, 2000 Search Engine www.albany.edu/sourcebook/

Uniform Crime Report (FBI 2001). "This report is based upon the reports of agencies that submitted 3-6 compatible months of data from January through June in both 2000 and 2001." FBI Press Release, December 17, 2001.

- Uniform Crime Report www.fbi.gov/ucr/016mosprelim.pdf
- FBI Press Release www.fbi.gov/pressrel/pressrel01/01prelimcius.htm

DEATH PENALTY

Beyond Reason: The Death Penalty and Offenders With Mental Retardation (HRW 2001). In this report, the Human Rights Watch reviews the issues surrounding the execution of the mentally retarded. It examines current definitions of mental retardation, legal standards, international human rights law, and specific capital cases.

- Beyond Reason: The Death Penalty and Offenders With Mental Retardation www.hrw.org/reports/2001/ustat/

Broken System: Error Rates in Capital Cases, 1973-1995 (Columbia University 2000). The Liebman study showed that more than two-thirds of death sentences have been overturned due to unreliable evidence or procedural violations at trial.

- Broken System: Error Rates in Capital Cases, 1973-1995 justice.policy.net/jpreport/index.html

Capital Punishment 2000 (BJS 2001). This report describes the characteristics of persons on death row and those executed in 2000. Preliminary data on executions in 2001 include state, method used and race of inmate.

- Capital Punishment 2000
www.ojp.usdoj.gov/bjs/abstract/cp00.htm

Capital Punishment 1999 (BJS 2000). This report describes the characteristics of persons on death row and those executed in 1999. Preliminary data on executions in 2000 include state, method used and race of inmate.

- Capital Punishment 1999
www.ojp.usdoj.gov/bjs/abstract/cp99.htm

Capital Punishment in New York State: Statistics from Six Years of Representation (NYCDO 2001). This report by the Capital Defender Office offers statistics showing how the death penalty has been implemented in New York State. The statistics show the number of capital and death-eligible cases, geographic differences in the application of the death penalty, race and gender information, and the duration of capital and noncapital cases in New York.

- Capital Punishment in New York State: Statistics from Six Years of Representation
www.nycdo.org/6yr.html

Death Penalty in Texas (Texas Civil Rights Project 2000). "This report pulls together in one place all the studies that exist with respect to the Texas capital punishment system, as well as various studies that deal with the administration of capital punishment overall in the nation."

- Death Penalty in Texas
www.igc.org/tcrp/downloads/Death_Penalty_Report/deathpenaltyreport.htm

Death Penalty Information Center Year End Report 2001 (DPIC 2001). The "Death Penalty Information Center's 2001 Year End Report found a 22% decline in executions, a drop in public support for capital punishment, and a steady stream of successful reform efforts throughout the nation last year. The review also notes that questions of fairness and a growing national concern about the application of the death penalty continue to shape America's capital punishment debate." *2001 Death Penalty Report Finds 22% Decline in Executions, Reform Initiatives Gaining Ground*, DPIC Press Release, December 13, 2001.

- Death Penalty Information Center Year End Report www.deathpenaltyinfo.org/YearEndReport2001.pdf
- 2001 Death Penalty Report Finds 22% Decline in Executions, Reform Initiatives Gaining Ground www.deathpenaltyinfo.org/PR-PICYREND2001.html

Death Row Roll Call: March 2000. The Nation has begun publishing a monthly list of pending executions in the United States derived from the Death Penalty Information Center.

- Death Row Roll Call: March 2000 www.thenation.com/deathrow/
- The Nation www.thenation.com/
- Death Penalty Information Center www.deathpenaltyinfo.org/

Death Row USA (NAACP Legal Defense Fund 2001). This is a quarterly report by the Criminal Justice Project of the NAACP Legal Defense and Education Fund providing statistical information on death row inmates, developments in Supreme Court cases and complete retrospective data on executions since the reinstatement of the death penalty.

- Death Row USA www.deathpenaltyinfo.org/DEATHROWUSArecent.pdf

Death Without Justice: A Guide for Examining the Administration of the Death Penalty in the United States (ABA 2001). The American Bar Association Section of Individual Rights and Responsibilities prepared this publication "to help jurisdictions that authorize the death penalty conduct comprehensive reviews of the laws, processes, and procedures relevant to the administration of capital punishment in their jurisdictions." For more information about the report, read Reviewing Death Penalty Policies and Procedures, ABA News Release, July 30, 2001

- Death Without Justice: A Guide for Examining the Administration of the Death Penalty in the United States www.abanet.org/irr/finaljune28.pdf
- Reviewing Death Penalty Polices and Procedures www.abanet.org/media/jul01/protocols.html

Dying Twice: Conditions on New York's Death Row (ABCNY 2001). The Bar Association's Committee on Corrections and the Committee on Capital Punishment conducted a joint study to assess and report on the conditions under which death row prisoners await execution in New York prisons.

- Dying Twice: Conditions on New York's Death Row www.abcny.org/currenarticle/dying%20 twice2.html

Federal Death Penalty System: Supplementary Data, Analysis and Revised Protocols for Capital Case Review (DOJ 2001). "The proportion of minority defendants in federal capital cases exceeds the proportion of minority individuals in the general population. The information gathered by the Department [of Justice] indicates that the cause of this disproportion is not racial or ethnic bias, but the representation of minorities in the pool of potential federal capital cases."

- Federal Death Penalty System: Supplementary Data, Analysis and Revised Protocols for Capital Case Review www.usdoj.gov/dag/pubdoc/deathpenaltystudy.htm

Gathering Momentum: The Continuing Impact of the American Bar Association Call for a Moratorium on Executions (ABA 2000) and Executive Summary published by the ABA's Section of Individual Rights and Responsibilities reveals a growing trend toward halting the death penalty due to the abysmal state of procedural fairness in capital cases. New ABA Report Reveals Growing Uneasiness With Administration of the Death Penalty, ABA Press Release, February 2, 2000.

- Gathering Momentum: The Continuing Impact of the American Bar Association Call for a Moratorium on Executions www.abanet.org/ftp/pub/irr/Final_Report_1-24-00.doc
- New ABA Report Reveals Growing Uneasiness With Administration of the Death Penalty www.abanet.org/irr/

Illusion of Control (AI 2001). This report concerns consensual executions of death row prisoners who have abandoned their appeals and "ask" to be put to death. Almost a hundred such executions have been carried out since 1977. "Consensual" Executions, Timothy McVeigh, and the Brutalizing Futility of the Death Penalty, AI Press Release, April 24, 2001

- Illusion of Control web.amnesty.org/ai.nsf/Index/AMR510532001?OpenDocument&of=COUNTRIES\\USA
- "Consensual" Executions, Timothy McVeigh, and the Brutalizing Futility of the Death Penalty www.web.amnesty.org/web/news.nsf/WebAll/6905A30CEE5C6647802

56A320052DDD4?Open Document

Mandatory Justice: Eighteen Reforms to the Death Penalty (Constitution Project 2001). "[T]he report details eighteen specific recommendations that relate to various aspects of capital punishment. Among other things, the reforms call for adequate compensation, standards and training for defense counsel; the removal of certain classes of defendants and homicides from death penalty eligibility; greater flexibility for introducing evidence that casts doubt on a conviction or sentence; gathering of data on the role of race in capital punishment and involvement of all races in the decision-making process; elimination of a judge's ability to impose a death sentence despite a jury recommendation for life imprisonment; and requiring prosecutors to open their files to the defense in death penalty cases."

- Mandatory Justice: Eighteen Reforms to the Death Penalty
www.constitutionproject.org/dpi/MandatoryJustice.pdf

Old Habits Die Hard: The Death Penalty in Oklahoma (AI 2001). This report focuses on the realities of death penalty procedures in Oklahoma. "Oklahoma's relentless pursuit of death sentences is in stark contrast to the global abolitionist trend. Moreover, the state frequently violates international safeguards governing the use of the death penalty, for example by executing the mentally impaired." Old Habits Die Hard: New Amnesty International Report on Death Penalty in Oklahoma, AI Press Release, April 26, 2001

- Old Habits Die Hard: The Death Penalty in Oklahoma
web.amnesty.org/ai.nsf/Index/AMR510552001?OpenDocument&of=COUNTRIES\\USA
- Old Habits Die Hard: New Amnesty International Report on

Death Penalty in Oklahoma
www.web.amnesty.org/web/news.nsf/weball/A076C4506F608D1880256A33003A9318

Survey of the Federal Death Penalty System: A Statistical Survey 1988-2000 (DOJ 2000). "This Survey provides information regarding the federal death penalty system since the enactment of the first modern capital punishment statute in 1988. The Survey explains the Department of Justice's internal decision-making process for deciding whether to seek the death penalty in individual cases, and presents statistical information focusing on the racial/ethnic and geographic distribution of defendants and their victims at particular stages of that decision-making process."

- Survey of the Federal Death Penalty System: A Statistical Survey 1988-2000
  www.usdoj.gov/dag/pubdoc/dpsurvey.html

Too Young to Vote, Old Enough to Be Executed (AI 2001). This report addresses the execution of juveniles in the United States.

- Too Young to Vote, Old Enough to Be Executed
  web.amnesty.org/ai.nsf/Index/AMR511052001?OpenDocument&of=COUNTRIES\\USA

DNA

Improved Analysis of DNA Short Tandem Repeats With Time-of-Flight Mass Spectrometry (NIJ 2001). "[M]ass spectrometry can be a useful and effective means for high-throughput DNA analysis, and . . . it has the capabilities to meet the needs of the forensic DNA community for offender DNA databases."

- Improved Analysis of DNA Short Tandem Repeats With Time-of-Flight Mass Spectrometry
  www.ncjrs.org/txtfiles1/nij/188292.txt

National Commission on the Future of DNA Evidence (NIJ 1999) was established to "maximize the value of forensic DNA evidence in the criminal justice system." Its web site contains publications and transcripts of Commission meetings concerning the potential uses of DNA testing.

- National Commission on the Future of DNA Evidence www.ojp.usdoj.gov/nij/dna/welcome.html

Reference Guide on DNA Evidence from <u>Reference Manual on Scientific Evidence</u> (FJC 2nd ed. 2000) is part of a federal judicial guide for evaluating scientific evidence that contains an informative review of DNA evidence.

- Reference Guide on DNA Evidence air.fjc.gov/public/pdf.nsf/lookup/sciman09.pdf/$file/sciman09.pdf
- Reference Manual on Scientific Evidence air.fjc.gov/public/fjcweb.nsf/pages/16

Survey of DNA Crime Laboratories (BJS 1998) is a study of publicly operated forensic laboratory workloads, budgets and operating procedures.

- Survey of DNA Crime Laboratories www.ojp.usdoj.gov/bjs/abstract/sdnacl98.htm

Understanding DNA Evidence: A Guide for Victim Service Providers (OVC 2001). "DNA evidence is playing a larger role than ever before in criminal cases throughout the country, both to convict the guilty and exonerate the wrongly accused. Biological samples that were impossible to test for DNA 10 years ago may yield critical evidence if tested today. Because DNA evidence is a powerful tool in the search for truth, it is important that victim service providers understand the potential significance of DNA evidence in their clients' cases."

- Understanding DNA Evidence: A Guide for Victim Service Providers www.ojp.usdoj.gov/ovc/publications/bulletins/dna_4_2001/welcome.html

What Every Law Enforcement Officer Should Know About DNA Evidence (NIJ 1999) is a basic review of DNA evidence collection guidelines.

- What Every Law Enforcement Officer Should Know About DNA Evidence www.ncjrs.org/pdffiles1/nij/bc000614.pdf

DRUG COURTS

Confronting the Cycle of Addiction and Recidivism: A Report to Chief Judge Judith S. Kaye by the New York State Commission on Drugs and the Courts (OCA 2000). Among the commission's recommendations for addressing the increasing number of drug offenses in the criminal justice system was the implementation of drug courts and drug treatment alternatives statewide.

- Confronting the Cycle of Addiction and Recidivism www.courts.state.ny.us/addictionrecidivism62000.html

Drug Testing in a Drug Court Environment (OJP 2000). This paper addresses "the most frequent issues that have been raised by drug court programs regarding drug testing. Although this report is by no means a definitive treatment of all of these issues, it is intended to provide an overview for drug court program officials—primarily lay persons—regarding the most critical topics that need to be addressed in developing and maintaining a drug testing capability."

- Drug Testing in a Drug Court Environment www.ncjrs.org/pdffiles1/ojp/181103.pdf

Evaluation of the D.C. Superior Court Drug Intervention Programs (NIJ 2000). "An evaluation of the impact of two D.C. Superior Court experimental interventions on drug-involved defendants in Washington."

- Evaluation of the D.C. Superior Court Drug Intervention Programs www.ncjrs.org/pdffiles1/nij/178941.pdf

Rebirth of Rehabilitation: Promise and Perils of Drug Courts (NIJ 2000). This report is "framed by an exploration of the possibilities drug courts offer for improving public safety and the pitfalls they may face. It is set in the context of the shift away from indeterminate sentencing, which occurred about the same time strong, empirically based evidence of the link between drugs and crime and the efficacy of treatment was coming to light."

- Rebirth of Rehabilitation: Promise and Perils of Drug Courts

www.ncjrs.org/pdffiles1/nij/181412.pdf

Research on Drug Courts: A Critical Review (CASA 2001). "This is a critical review of 37 published and unpublished evaluations of drug courts (including seven juvenile drug courts, one DUI court, and one family drug court) produced between 1999 and April 2001. . . . Drug courts have achieved considerable local support and have provided intensive, long-term treatment services to offenders with long histories of drug use and criminal justice contacts, previous treatment failures, and high rates of health and social problems."

- Research on Drug Courts: A Critical Review www.casacolumbia.org/usr_doc/researchondrug.pdf

Treatment Alternatives in the Criminal Court: A Process Evaluation of the Bronx County Drug Court (VIJ 2001). This is a report on the implementation evaluation of the Bronx Treatment Court in its first 18 months of operation.

- Treatment Alternatives in the Criminal Court www.vera.org/publicatio ns/publications_2c.asp? publication_id=19&publ ication_content_id=58& section_id=16&project_i d=&sub_section_id=5

Treatment Services in Adult Drug Courts: Report on the 1999 National Drug Court Treatment Survey (OJP 2001). "The results of this national survey show clearly that treatment services designed for and used by drug courts comport with scientifically established principles of treatment effectiveness. . . . The standards promulgated in these documents present succinct descriptions of treatment delivery methods that have been effective with offender and other populations and serve as a guide to present survey findings in the context of effective professional practices."

- Treatment Services in Adult Drug Courts: Report on the 1999 National Drug Court Treatment Survey www.ncjrs.org/txtfiles1/ ojp/188086.txt

What We Know About the Impact of Drug Courts (CJRI 2000). This is the testimony of John S. Goldkamp, Professor of Criminal Justice, Temple University, before the Senate Judiciary Committee on Youth Violence, in which he reviewed the impacts of drug courts and research into their effectiveness.

- What We Know About the Impact of Drug Courts www.cjri.com/pdf/testi mony.pdf

DRUG LAWS

Color Test Reagents/Kits for Preliminary Identification of Drugs of Abuse NIJ Standard-0604.01 (NIJ 2000) "The purpose of this standard is to establish minimum requirements for color test reagent/kits to detect drugs of abuse and methods of testing the reagents to determine compliance with those requirements. This standard applies to field-testing kits that consist of color test reagents for the preliminary identification of drugs of abuse in their pure and/or diluted forms. It does not apply to kits that use thin layer chromatography as the identification procedure nor to kits that identify drugs in body fluids."

- Color Test Reagents/Kits for Preliminary Identification of Drugs of Abuse NIJ Standard-0604.01
www.ncjrs.org/pdffiles1/nij/183258.pdf

Drug and Crime Facts (BJS 2001) summarizes U.S. statistics about drug-related crimes, law enforcement, courts, and corrections from a variety of sources.

- Drug and Crime Facts
www.ojp.usdoj.gov/bjs/dcf/contents.htm

Drug Offense Cases in Juvenile Courts 1989-1998 (OJJDP 2001). "This Fact Sheet discusses drug abuse violations as the criminal offense category with the highest arrest rate in 1999."

- Drug Offense Cases in Juvenile Courts 1989-1998
www.ncjrs.org/pdffiles1/ojjdp/fs200136.pdf

Drug Policy Project (King County Bar Association, WA 2001). The goal of the Project is to find the best long-term approach to controlling drug abuse. They have issued several reports, including one on Use of Criminal Sanctions.

- Drug Policy Project
www.kcba.org/drug_law/druglaw_index.htm
- Use of Criminal Sanctions
www.kcba.org/drug_law/criminal.htm

Drug Use and Justice: An Examination of California Drug Policy Enforcement (Justice Policy

Institute 2000). This report examined the results of years of increasing arrests and prison sentences for drug related offenses in California and the impact of drug enforcement policy on the crime rate.

- Drug Use and Justice: An Examination of California Drug Policy Enforcement www.cjcj.org/cadrug/cadrug.html

Federal Drug Offenders, 1999 With Trends, 1984-1999 (BJS 2001). "Describes offenders investigated for and charged with Federal drug offenses during 1999. This report includes statistics describing type of drug involved in the offense, criminal history of defendants charged, demographic characteristics of defendants charged, defendants' role in the drug conspiracy, and sentences imposed. Also included are statistics describing the change in the number of suspects investigated, prosecuted, proportion sentenced to prison, and time to be served for the period 1984 through 1999."

- Federal Drug Offenders, 1999 With Trends, 1984-1999 www.ojp.usdoj.gov/bjs/abstract/fdo99.htm

Punishment and Prejudice: Racial Disparities in the War on Drugs (HRW 2000) is a statistical study showing the disparate impact of drug laws and sentences based on race.

- Punishment and Prejudice: Racial Disparities in the War on Drugs www.hrw.org/reports/2000/usa/

"Stupid and Irrational and Barbarous": New York Judges Speak Against the Rockefeller Drug Laws (CANY 2001). "More and more judges are adding their critical voices to the debate about the mandatory sentencing provisions of the Rockefeller Drug Laws. The following is a sample of what some have said over the years about these statutes when they have had to apply them in trial court or in the appellate courts. The report concludes with relevant comments judges have made about these laws in settings outside the courtroom."

- "Stupid and Irrational and Barbarous": New York Judges Speak Against the Rockefeller Drug Laws www.droptherock.org/Judges_Report.htm

Trace Detection of Narcotics Using a Preconcentrator/Ion Mobility Spectrometer System (NIJ 2001). "This report discusses work performed in the area of trace drug detection. . . . The overall goal of these studies was to investigate the efficacy of the preconcentrator in the general field of drug detection. In addition, it was hoped to make an initial determination concerning the feasibility of a trace drug detection portal for personnel screening that would operate on the same principles as the explosives detection portal."

- Trace Detection of Narcotics Using a Preconcentrator/Ion Mobility Spectrometer System www.ncjrs.org/txtfiles1/nij/187111.txt

DWI

Horizontal Gaze Nystagmus the Science and the Law: A Resource Guide for Judges, Prosecutors, and Law Enforcement (NHTSA 2001). "[T]his guide provides an overview of the science supporting the [Horizontal Gaze Nystagmus] HGN test as a valid indicator of impairment, distinguishes between HGN and other forms of nystagmus, and provides the necessary tools to establish admissibility of the HGN test in court."

- Horizontal Gaze Nystagmus the Science and the Law: A Resource Guide for Judges, Prosecutors, and Law Enforcement www.nhtsa.dot.gov/people/injury/enforce/nystagmus/

State Alcohol Law is a database of state laws concerning the distribution, taxation, sale, and consumption of alcoholic beverages including criminal and civil liability. The site is maintained by the Alcohol Epidemiology Program at the University of Minnesota, Minneapolis.

- State Alcohol Law
  www.epi.umn.edu/enacted/

EXPERTS
CPA Directory (CPA Directory.com). This is one of the largest CPA directories on the web. Information about licensure, accounting news and related resources are also listed here.

- CPA Directory
  cpadirectory.com/

EYEWITNESS EVIDENCE
Attorney General Guidelines for Preparing and Conducting Photo and Live Lineup Identification Procedures (NJ Dept of Law and Public Safety 2001) contains New Jersey's newly adopted rules for conducting identification proceedings based on federal guidelines, including the use of sequential lineups.

- Attorney General Guidelines for Preparing and Conducting Photo and Live Lineup Identification Procedures
  www.state.nj.us/lps/dcj/agguide/photoid.pdf

Eyewitness Evidence: A Guide for Law Enforcement (NIJ 1999) is intended to provide local law enforcement with recommendations for improving the accuracy and fairness of identification proceedings, including the use of sequential lineups.

- Eyewitness Evidence: A Guide for Law Enforcement
  www.ncjrs.org/pdffiles1/nij/178240.pdf

Model Identification Rules: An Act to Improve the Accuracy of Eyewitness Identification Procedures (American Psychology Law Society) is a proposed statute, the Eyewitness Identification Act, intended to promote accurate identification of suspects and reduce the risk of misidentification and wrongful conviction.

- Model Identification Rules: An Act to Improve the Accuracy of Eyewitness Identification Procedures
www.unl.edu/apls/Modelact.htm

FEDERAL COURTS
Courts Shift to E-Filings
Federal Computer Week, December 5, 2001 discusses the new rules that permit pleadings to be filed in federal court electronically, including email.

- Courts Shift to E-Filings
www.fcw.com/fcw/articles/2001/1203/webcourts-12-05-01.asp

CourtWeb (USDC) is a free court sponsored service that provides access to select federal district court decisions from the Southern and Northern Districts of New York and several other participating federal trial courts. The search engine allows users to search by judge, case number, date, case title or full-text.

- CourtWeb
www.nysd.uscourts.gov/rulings.htm

U.S. Circuit Court of Appeals Search Engine (LII 2001). The Legal Information Institute has created a search engine for its collection of federal circuit court decisions. Courts may be searched individually or in toto. The scope of the collection varies from cases beginning in 1992 for the Fifth Circuit to the most current decisions from all the circuits.

- U.S. Circuit Court of Appeals Search Engine
www.law.cornell.edu:9999/USCA-ALL/results.html
- Legal Information Institute at Cornell University School of Law
www.law.cornell.edu

U.S. Supreme Court. This is the official United States Supreme Court site on which they post their most recent full text opinions as well as administrative information.

- U.S. Supreme Court
  www.supremecourtus.gov

FEDERAL PRACTICE

Federal Grand Jury is a resource page created by two law professors who are experts on how federal grand juries operate and the role they play in federal law enforcement. It includes links to information on New York grand jury practice.

- Federal Grand Jury
  www.udayton.edu/~grandjur/

Reversible Errors 1995-2000 (Editor: Alexander Bunin, Federal Public Defender Northern New York and Vermont). This is a well-organized collection of court decisions in which a criminal defendant received relief from a U.S. Court of Appeals or the U.S. Supreme Court.

- Reversible Errors 1995-1999
  www.crimelynx.com/00errors.html

United States Attorney's Manual (DOJ 2001) is the official handbook of federal prosecutors. The online version is searchable and each title is downloadable. It contains general policies and some procedures relevant to the work of the United States Attorneys' offices and to their relations with the legal divisions, investigative agencies, and other components within the Department of Justice. Most notable for practitioners is <u>Title 9: Criminal Division</u>.

- United States Attorney's Manual
  www.usdoj.gov/usao/eousa/foia_reading_room/usam/index.htm
- Title 9: Criminal Division
  www.usdoj.gov/usao/eousa/foia_reading_room/usam/title9/title9.htm

FEDERAL SENTENCING

Federal Sentencing Guideline Manual (USSC 2001). This web site contains the contents of the complete official federal sentencing guidelines. Supplements and updates can be found on the United States Sentencing Commission web site.

- 2001 Federal Sentencing Guideline Manual www.ussc.gov/2001guid/TABCON01.htm
- United States Sentencing Commission www.ussc.gov

Federal Sentencing Guideline Materials (Whitehorse Solutions 2001) Whitehorse Solutions sells software for calculating sentences under the Federal Guidelines. In addition, their web site contains many full text documents related to the federal sentencing laws.

- Federal Sentencing Guidelines Materials www.whitehorsesolutions.com/fsglaw/

Sentencing Decisions of the Second Circuit (Mischel, Neuman and Horn 2001) is a new newsletter published by a private firm, Mischel, Neuman and Horn, which contains summaries of recent decisions and is organized by topic.

- Sentencing Decisions of the Second Circuit www.mnhappeals.com/newslett.htm

Sentencing Guidelines: Reflections on the Future (NIJ 2001). This report is a review and evaluation of the sentencing guidelines movement. It considers the interaction of the guidelines with current concepts such as restorative justice and get-tough on crime policies.

- Sentencing Guidelines: Reflections on the Future www.ncjrs.org/pdffiles1/nij/186480.pdf

FORENSICS

Best Practices for Seizing Electronic Evidence (U.S. Secret Service 2001) This is a manual designed to assist law enforcement in understanding the basics of handling and preserving electronic evidence.

- Best Practices for Seizing Electronic Evidence
www.treas.gov/usss/index.htm?electronic_evidence.htm&1

Biometrics Catalog (NIJ 2001). Biometrics are automated methods of recognizing a person based on physiological or behavioral characteristics, e.g., fingerprinting, retinal scan, face and voice recognition. The Biometrics Catalog was developed as a service to the biometrics community and as part of the Counterdrug Technology Information Network. It can be searched using multiple fields or keyword.

- Biometrics Catalog
www.biometricscatalog.org/

Computer Crime and Intellectual Property Section (DOJ). The United States Department of Justice has created a web site with resources devoted to investigating computer crime, including Federal Guidelines for Searching and Seizing Computers.

- Computer Crime and Intellectual Property Section
www.cybercrime.gov/
- Federal Guidelines for Searching and Seizing Computers
www.cybercrime.gov/searching.html

Crime Scene Investigation: A Guide for Law Enforcement (NIJ 1999) is a guide intended for use by law enforcement and others who have responsibility for protecting crime scenes, preserving physical evidence, and collecting and submitting the evidence for scientific examination.

- Crime Scene Investigation: A Guide for Law Enforcement
www.ncjrs.org/pdffiles1/nij/178280.pdf

Death Investigation: A Guide for the Scene Investigator (NIJ 1999) is a set of standards to provide a uniform approach for homicide investigations.

- Death Investigation: A Guide for the Scene Investigator ncjrs.org/pdffiles/167568.pdf

Electronic Crime Scene Investigation: A Guide for First Responders (NIJ 2001). "The law enforcement response to electronic evidence requires that officers, investigators, forensic examiners, and managers all play a role. This document serves as a guide for the first responder. A first responder may be responsible for the recognition, collection, preservation, transportation, and/or storage of electronic evidence."

- Electronic Crime Scene Investigation: A Guide for First Responders www.ncjrs.org/pdffiles1/nij/187736.pdf

Fingerprints: The Origins of Crime Detection and the Murder Case That Launched Forensic Science (Hyperion 2001) and **Suspect Identities: A History of Fingerprinting and Criminal Identification** (Harvard University Press 2001) are two books on the history and development of fingerprint identification. The latter book contains a chapter, "Fraud, Fabrication, and False Positives," about the reliability and quality of fingerprint evidence.

- Fingerprints: The Origins of Crime Detection and the Murder Case That Launched Forensic Science (Publisher's Site) www.hyperionbooks.com/books/2001spring/fingerprints.htm
- Fingerprints: The Origins of Crime Detection and the Murder Case That Launched Forensic Science (Author Site) www.fingerprintbook.com/
- Suspect Identities: A History of Fingerprinting and Criminal Identi-

fication
www.hup.harvard.edu/Newsroom/pr_suspect_ident.htm

Fire and Arson Scene Evidence: A Guide for Public Safety Personnel (NIJ 2000) discusses procedures for locating and preserving evidence in fire and arson investigations.

- Fire and Arson Scene Evidence: A Guide for Public Safety Personnel
www.ncjrs.org/pdffiles1/nij/181584.pdf

Guide for Explosion and Bombing Scene Investigation (NIJ 2000) is a description of the proper procedures to be followed in locating and collecting evidence at the site of an explosion.

- Guide for Explosion and Bombing Scene Investigation
www.ncjrs.org/pdffiles1/nij/181869.pdf

Handbook of Forensic Services (FBI 1999). This Handbook contains the procedures and policies for identifying, collecting and preserving forensic evidence. It also includes information about the tests conducted by the FBI Laboratory.

- Handbook of Forensic Services
www.fbi.gov/hq/lab/handbook/intro.htm

National Conference on Science and the Law Proceedings (NIJ 2000). Scientists, attorneys, and judges, address the relationship between science and law.

- National Conference on Science and the Law
www.ncjrs.org/pdffiles1/nij/179630.pdf

Resource Guide to Law Enforcement, Corrections and Forensics Technologies (NIJ 2001). "The Guide is designed for local administrators who need a ready reference to help them make informed decisions when acquiring current and emerging technologies."

- Resource Guide to Law Enforcement, Corrections and Forensics Technologies
  www.ncjrs.org/txtfiles1/nij/186822.txt

Science, Technology and the Law Resource Center (NCSC 2001). The National Center for State Courts created a resource center to assist judges, law clerks, and court staff in addressing state-of-the art science and technology issues reflected in the cases on their dockets.

- Science, Technology and the Law Resource Center
  www.ncsc.dni.us/RESEARCH/ST&L/index.html

Sexual Assault Nurse Examiner (SANE) Programs (OVC 2001). "A SANE is a registered nurse (R.N.) who has advanced education and clinical preparation in forensic examination of sexual assault victims . . . Those who work with sexual assault victims have long recognized that victims are often retraumatized when they come to hospital emergency departments for medical care and forensic evidence collection."

- Sexual Assault Nurse Examiner (SANE) Programs
  www.ojp.usdoj.gov/ovc/publications/bulletins/sane_4_2001/welcome.html

FORMS

FedForms (FirstGov) is a site that collects links to the most commonly requested government agency forms. Federal forms not available here can be found through links to other sites appearing on FedForms. Forms can be searched by agency or keyword with direct links to the host site.

- FedForms
  www.fedforms.gov/

U.S. Court Forms (American Legalnet 2001) is a service that offers access to thousands of federal and state government forms for free. Interactive forms are also available for subscribers to the service for a fee. For more information, read Company Moves to Capitalize on E-Filing, Federal Computer Week, February 26, 2001.

- U.S. Court Forms www.uscourtforms.com/
- Company Moves to Capitalize on E-Filing www.civic.com/civic/articles/2001/0226/webcourt-02-26-01.asp

IMMIGRATION

Asylumlaw.org is devoted to helping lawyers prepare asylum cases. This site contains legal news, forms, briefs, referrals and many more resources.

- Asylumlaw.org www.asylumlaw.org/

INTERPRETERS

L and H Online Translations, featured on Microsoft Office Update, is a software translating program provided by Lernout and Hauspie, who create and market translation software products that will convert English text to French, German, Japanese, Spanish, Italian and Portuguese and vice versa.

- L and H Online Translations translate.lhsl.com/
- Lernout and Hauspie www.lhsl.com/default2.htm

Language Line Services offers phone access to translators in over 140 languages. They have experience working in different settings including the criminal justice system. As part of the Interpreting Justice Partnership between Language Line and the National Legal Aid and Defender Association (NLADA) special subscription pricing is available.

- Language Line Services www.languageline.com
- National Legal Aid and Defender Association www.nlada.org

WordReference is an Internet tool for translating Spanish, French, Italian and German words into English. Dictionary tools for each language can be inserted into a web browser as a link button, then any highlighted word on a web page can be translated into English.

- WordReference
  www.wordreference.com/english/InstallIEnew.htm

INVESTIGATIVE TOOLS

John E. Reid and Associates is a private investigation and consulting service that posts valuable articles about investigation and interrogation techniques.

- John E. Reid and Associates
  www.reid.com/materials-tip-mar01.html

Social Security Death Index, accessible through Ancestry.com, offers a database with information provided by the Social Security Administration through the end of September 2001 and contains 66,668,463 names. Its search options include date of birth and last known residence.

- Social Security Death Index
  www.ancestry.com/search/rectype/vital/ssdi/main.htm
- Ancestry.com
  www.ancestry.com

JURY INSTRUCTIONS

ForeCite: Criminal Jury Instructions Products and Materials. ForeCite contains an assortment of resources on jury instructions and new developments, along with information about their CD-ROM products, including Electronic Jury Instruction Practice Manual for Criminal Law Practitioners in Every State and Federal Jurisdiction.

- ForeCite: Criminal Jury Instructions Products and Materials
  www.juryinstructions.com/criminal_home_page.htm
- Electronic Jury Instruction Practice Manual for Criminal Law Practitioners in Every State and Federal Jurisdiction
  www.juryinstructions.com/50_plus_home.htm

Insider's Guide to Criminal Justice Resources

Presumption of Innocence and Proof Beyond a Reasonable Doubt (OCA 2000) are the latest versions of the revisions to the New York Criminal Jury Instructions.

- Presumption of Innocence and Proof Beyond a Reasonable Doubt www.courts.state.ny.us/cji/bard.html

What is the Law? - Finding Jury Instructions LLRX, November 15, 2000 is an article describing the sources for civil and criminal jury instructions in various states available on the web.

- What is the Law? - Finding Jury Instructions www.llrx.com/columns/reference19.htm

JUVENILE JUSTICE

Appropriate and Effective Use of Security Technologies in U.S. Schools (NIJ 1999). This report responded to the need to provide schools with research into the causes of school violence and to lay the groundwork for prevention programs.

- Appropriate and Effective Use of Security Technologies in U.S. Schools www.ncjrs.org/school/home.html

Breaking the Juvenile Drug-Crime Cycle (NIJ 2001). This report "summarizes existing knowledge about programs designed to intervene in the juvenile drug-crime cycle and, based on that knowledge, identifies interventions that published research judges to offer the best chances for success. It also provides guidelines and recommendations for developing a comprehensive juvenile justice system that can best address the needs of drug-using juvenile offenders."

- Breaking the Juvenile Drug-Crime Cycle www.ncjrs.org/txtfiles1/nij/186156.txt

Changing the PINS System in New York (VIJ

2001). "This study examines the strengths and weaknesses of the current Persons in Need of Supervision (PINS) system and provides the first comprehensive projections of how many more children will enter under the new law."

- Changing the PINS System in New York
www.vera.org/publications/publications_2c.asp?publication_id=130&publication_content_id=155&section_id=16&project_id=&sub_section_id=5

Delinquency Cases in Juvenile Courts, 1998 (OJJDP 2001). "Presents statistics related to delinquency cases processed by U.S. juvenile courts in 1998. Drawing on data from almost 2,100 courts with jurisdiction over nearly 70 percent of the U.S. juvenile population, this Fact Sheet highlights various aspects of delinquency cases, including gender, age, race, detention, intake, waiver, and adjudication and disposition."

- Delinquency Cases in Juvenile Courts, 1998
www.ncjrs.org/pdffiles1/ojjdp/fs200131.pdf

Delinquency Cases Waived to Criminal Court, 1989-1998 (OJJDP 2001). "This Fact Sheet presents estimates of the number of cases transferred from juvenile court to criminal court through the judicial waiver mechanism between 1989 and 1998. These estimates are based on data from nearly 2,100 jurisdictions, representing almost 70% of the U.S. juvenile population (youth age 10 through the upper age of original juvenile court jurisdiction in each State)."

- Delinquency Cases Waived to Criminal Court, 1989-1998
www.ncjrs.org/pdffiles1/ojjdp/fs200135.pdf

Florida Experiment: An Analysis of the Impact of Granting Prosecutors Discretion to Try Juveniles as Adults (Justice Policy Institute 1999).

Florida ranks highest among states that try juveniles as adults and many are questioning the wisdom of vesting that discretionary choice with the prosecutor.

- Florida Experiment: An Analysis of the Impact of Granting Prosecutors Discretion to Try Juveniles as Adults
www.cjcj.org/florida/

Justice by Gender: The Lack of Appropriate Prevention, Diversion and Treatment Alternatives for Girls in the Juvenile Justice System (ABA 2001) is a report on the current state of girls in the juvenile justice system and a starting point for a dialogue on the specific issues they face. "A fundamental issue underlying this report is whether the growth in the number of girls in the delinquency system is a result of an increase in their violent and aggressive behavior. Although further research into this proposition is required, preliminary studies suggest that what has changed is our response to their behavior."

- Justice by Gender: The Lack of Appropriate Prevention, Diversion and Treatment Alternatives for Girls in the Juvenile Justice System
www.abanet.org/crimjust/juvjus/girls.html

Juvenile Arrests 1999 (OJJDP 2000) "Provides a summary and analysis of national and State juvenile arrest data reported in the FBI's October 2000 report, Crime in the United States, 1999."

- Juvenile Arrests 1999
www.ncjrs.org/pdffiles1/ojjdp/185236.pdf

Juveniles Facing Criminal Sanctions: Three States That Changed the Rules (OJJDP 2000). This is a federal study of the juvenile justice systems in three states, Wisconsin, New Mexico, and Minnesota, which highlights the need for change.

- Juveniles Facing Criminal Sanctions: Three States That Changed the Rules
ojjdp.ncjrs.org/pubs/181203

Juveniles in Adult Prisons and Jails (BJA 2000). "This report provides data that are critical for an effective response to the growing number of juveniles being housed in adult jails and prisons. This report documents the number of youth in adult facilities as of 1998, their demographic and offense characteristics, the legal and administrative processes by which such commitments are permitted, the issues faced by adult correctional systems in managing juveniles, and the conditions of juveniles confined in adult facilities."

- Juveniles in Adult Prisons and Jails
www.ncjrs.org/txtfiles1/bja/182503.txt

Kids and Violence: A Resource Guide (MSNBC 1999) is a collection of articles and resources about violence among school age children.

- Kids and Violence: A Resource Guide
www.msnbc.com/news/297184.asp

Mental Health Initiatives (OJJDP 2001). "Researchers at Northwestern University Medical School in Chicago, IL, have been studying alcohol, drug, and mental disorders among a large sample of juvenile detainees in the Cook County Detention Center in Chicago since November 1995. With funding from OJJDP, other Federal agencies, and private foundations, a longitudinal component was added to this study in November 1998."

- Mental Health Initiatives
www.ncjrs.org/pdffiles1/ojjdp/fs200130.pdf

National Study Comparing the Environments of Boot Camps With Traditional Facilities for Juvenile Offenders (NIJ 2001). "The focus of the study described here was to compare boot camps with more traditional facilities by measuring conditions of the institutional environment."

- National Study Comparing the Environments of Boot Camps With Traditional Facilities for Juvenile Offenders
www.ncjrs.org/pdffiles1/nij/187680.pdf

No Minor Matter: Children in Maryland's Jails (HRW 1999). The problems of housing juvenile offenders in adult detention facilities and the overall policy of treating minors as adults is addressed in this report.

- No Minor Matter: Children in Maryland's Jails
www.hrw.org/reports/1999/maryland

Providing Effective Representation for Youth Prosecuted as Adults (BJA 2000). "This bulletin describes successes in public defenders' attempts to provide high-quality representation to youth prosecuted in adult criminal courts. It uses the experiences of defenders across the country to identify key elements of defender programs that effectively meet the needs of transferred children."

- Providing Effective Representation for Youth Prosecuted as Adults
www.ncjrs.org/pdffiles1/bja/182502.pdf

Restorative Justice Conferences as an Early Response to Young Offenders. (OJJDP 2001). "Describes restorative justice conferencing, a promising form of early intervention for very young offenders that brings together an offending youth, his or her victim, and supporters of both the offender and victim with a trained facilitator."

- Restorative Justice Conferences as an Early Response to Young Offenders
www.ncjrs.org/pdffiles1/ojjdp/187769.pdf

Study of Juvenile Transfers to Criminal Court in Florida (OJJDP 2001). "The project is assessing the impact of transfer laws and practices, including the effectiveness of using transfer as a crime control strategy."

- Study of Juvenile Transfers to Criminal Court in Florida
  www.ncjrs.org/txtfiles1/fs99113.txt

Victims, Judges, and Juvenile Court Reform Through Restorative Justice (OVC 2000). "For years, the juvenile justice system has focused one dimensionally on the needs and risks of offenders. As a result, the criminal justice system does not currently offer victims a 'level playing field.' Today, most juvenile justice systems need to give first and primary attention to increasing their responsiveness to the needs of crime victims. One way to accomplish this is for juvenile justice systems to adopt and apply the principles of restorative justice, which recognizes three stakeholders (or coparticipants) in any 'justice' process—the victim, the offender, and the community.... Four focus groups were held during the spring and summer of 1997, bringing together a total of 20 juvenile court judges and 18 crime victims to hear each other's perspectives about problems in juvenile court."

- Victims, Judges, and Juvenile Court Reform Through Restorative Justice
  www.ojp.usdoj.gov/ovc/publications/bulletins/vj_10_2000_2/welcome.html

Youth in the Criminal Justice System: Guidelines for Policymakers and Practitioners (ABA Criminal Justice Section 2001). These guidelines are intended to cover the policy, procedural, and programmatic implications of juveniles being transferred to the adult criminal justice system.

- Youth in the Criminal Justice System: Guidelines for Policymakers and Practitioners www.abanet.org/crimjust/pubs/reports/index.html

LAW OFFICE MANAGEMENT

Disaster/Business-Recovery Planning - Is Your Firm Ready?, New York Law Journal, November 5, 2001 is an article that outlines basic preparation and guidelines for weathering catastrophes while minimizing interruption of service to clients.

- Disaster/Business-Recovery Planning - Is Your Firm Ready? www6.law.com/lawcom/displayid.cfm?statename=NY&docnum=94459&table=news&flag=full

Do You Know What You Know?, AmTech Law, September 19, 2001 is a discussion on the value of knowledge management to law firms and a plan for creating a chief knowledge officer.

- Do You Know What You Know? www.law.com/cgi-bin/gx.cgi/AppLogic+FTContentServer?pagename=law/View&c=Article&cid=ZZZ1WHCQJRC&live=true&cst=6&pc=0&pa=0&s=News&ExpIgnore=true&showsummary=0

Every Firm Needs an Emergency Plan, LexisONE, September 14, 2001 reviews the steps a law firm can take to develop and implement a plan to weather the unexpected.

- Every Firm Needs an Emergency Plan www.lexisone.com/practicemanagement/pmlibrary/pm091401a.html

Five Myths of Case Management, American Lawyer Media, November 19, 2001 explores common misconceptions about the capabilities of case management systems. It then considers important points in developing a system that will meet expectations.

- Five Myths of Case Management

www.law.com/cgi-bin/gx.cgi/AppLogic+FTContentServer?pagename=law/View&c=Article&cid=ZZZQN4LJ1UC&live=true&cst=6&pc=0&pa=0&s=News&ExpIgnore=true&showsummary=0

Focus on Function, American Bar Association Journal, November 2001 offers insights into law firm design that works along functional lines and organizes office technology around specific areas of practice.

- Focus on Function
  www.abanet.org/journal/nov01/tkdave.html

Judgment Day, Legal Times, December 12, 2001 is an analysis of common pitfalls facing decision makers and ways to avoid them.

- Judgment Day
  www.law.com/cgi-bin/gx.cgi/AppLogic+FTContentServer?pagename=law/View&c=Article&cid=ZZZ1ZCPKOUC&live=true&cst=1&pc=0&pa=0&s=News&ExpIgnore=true&showsummary=0

Law Office Policy and Procedures Manual (ABA 4th ed. 2000) is a resource manual that provides information and forms for basic law office operating policies and procedures. It includes a diskette with all the essential forms from the manual. The new edition also includes sections on: sexual harassment; support staff responsibilities; personnel policies and benefits; Internet and video surveillance; and disaster recovery among other things.

- Law Office Policy and Procedures Manual
  www.abanet.org/lpm/catalog/511-0441.html

LegalBiz Online is a new web-based magazine launched by Martindale-Hubbell that features articles on legal marketing, law libraries, legal administration, law practice management, and new uses of technology in legal offices.

- LegalBiz Online www.martindale.com/xp/Martindale/Professional_Resources/LegalBiz_Online/legalbiz_online.xml

New York State Office of General Services' Procurement Services offers information concerning state contract awards and price structure for offices eligible to receive services at state contract rates.

- New York State Office of General Services' Procurement Services www.ogs.state.ny.us/purchase/default.asp

Virtual Law Office: The Busy Attorney's Guide, LLRX, October 15, 2001 discusses various techniques for attorneys who plan to work remotely or at home.

- Virtual Law Office: The Busy Attorney's Guide www.llrx.com/features/virtuallawoffice.htm

Writing for Clients, LexisONE, October 23, 2001, is an article that describes techniques for effectively communicating with and counseling clients in clear understandable language.

- Writing for Clients www.lexisone.com/professionaldevelopment/pdlibrary/pd102301d.html

LAW OFFICE TECHNOLOGY

Adobe Acrobat Legal Solutions is a compilation of resources about Adobe's latest PDF software, version 5.0, and its many applications to legal practice, including electronic filing.

- Adobe Acrobat Legal Solutions www.adobe.com/products/acrobat/legalsolutions.html

Battle of the Software Giants, Redux (July 16, 2001). Collection of articles from Law.com reviewing and comparing the latest versions of Microsoft Office and Corel's WordPerfect Office.

- Battle of the Software Giants, Redux
www.law.com/cgi-bin/gx.cgi/AppLogic+FTContentServer?pagename=law/View&c=Article&cid=ZZZYONU94PC&live=true&cst=6&pc=0&pa=0&s=News&ExpIgnore=true&showsummary=0
- Law.com
www.law.com/index.html

CNET Reviews 5 Online Answering Services presents a critical overview of unified messaging services that combine email addresses, fax numbers and voice mail into one account. These services offer a range of options for consolidating messages from different accounts into one place that can be accessed online.

- CNET Reviews 5 Online Answering Services
www.cnet.com/software/0-3227887-8-4797241-1.html

Create Adobe PDF Online is a web-based service to convert documents into Adobe PDF files. Free trial and subscription information are available.

- Create Adobe PDF Online
createpdf.adobe.com/index.pl/2448929265.71846?BP=IE

Data Recovery, LexisONE, September 25, 2001 is an article that describes practices and procedures for safeguarding and restoring law office computer files.

- Data Recovery
www.lexisone.com/practicemanagement/pmlibrary/pm092501b.html

Davis Polk Unplugged, AmTech Law, December 3, 2001 reviews the results of The American Lawyer's annual law firm technology survey, Tech Scorecard: Associates Rank Their Firms. It ranked law firms according to the associates' views of office technology, training, support and benefits to clients.

- Davis Polk Unplugged www.law.com/cgi-bin/gx.cgi/AppLogic+FTContentServer?pagename=law/View&c=Article&cid=ZZZVOL3LKUC&live=true&cst=6&pc=0&pa=0&s=News&ExpIgnore=true&showsummary=0
- Tech Scorecard: Associates Rank Their Firms www.law.com/special/professionals/2001/tech_scorecard.html

Finjan is a computer security software company that offers free web-based tests to illustrate the vulnerability of office computers. They sell a line of products designed to protect networks and web users against malicious codes and viruses that can enter through the web browser.

- Finjan www.finjan.com/mcrc/test.cfm

FreeAnswers.com enables users to solve computer-related problems by asking questions in everyday language. It provides access to knowledge bases from Microsoft, Adobe, Intuit and AutoDesk.

- FreeAnswers.com www.freeanswers.com/

GoToMyPC is a web-based tool for accessing computer files from any location. For a monthly fee, users can connect with their office or home computers through a web browser at another location. A review of this product and comparison to similar tools, such as PCAnywhere, can be found at CNET Review.

- GoToMyPC www.gotomypc.com/
- PCAnywhere www.symantec.com/pcanywhere/
- CNET Review swreviews.netscape.com/software/0-5421322-8-6601682-2.html?tag=st.sw.5421322-8-6601682-1.arrow.5421322-8-6601682-2

How Not to Commit Malpractice With Your Computer, LexisONE, September 25, 2001 describes issues related to computer security, data protection, secure email communications and other facets of maintaining confidential and quality work product in the law office.

- How Not to Commit Malpractice With Your Computer
  www.lexisone.com/pract icemanagement/pmlibra ry/pm092601a.html

Instant Messages Catch On in Legal Circles, American Lawyer Media, September 17, 2001 describes the benefits of instant messaging for cooperation and support among legal, support staff and outside experts and consultants. It also increases access to the office for lawyers on the road.

- Instant Messages Catch On in Legal Circles
  www.law.com/cgi-bin/gx.cgi/AppLogic+FT ContentServer?pagenam e=law/View&c=Article& cid=ZZZR2K8HJRC&liv e=true&cst=6&pc=0&pa =0&s=News&ExpIgnore =true&showsummary=0

Keeping Pace With the Changing Technology Scene, LLRX, September 3, 2001 is a thorough review of web sites offering current awareness information on developments in law-related technology.

- Keeping Pace With the Changing Technology Scene
  www.llrx.com/columns/ notes43.htm

Law Office Software Center is part of LexisONE's Legal Internet Guide. It contains links to many useful products ranging from case management to litigation support.

- Law Office Software Center
  www.lexisone.com/legal research/legalguide/law office_software/law_of fice_software_index.ht m
- Legal Internet Guide
  www.lexisone.com/legal research/legalguide/lega l_guide_index.html

Learn2Type is a web site that can measure your typing ability and provide lessons for learning or improving touch-typing skills. This service is free.

- Learn2Type
  www.learn2type.com/TypingTest

NetPost Mailing Online is a new service from the United States Post Office for sending mail, including certified mail through the web. Federal Files Go Digital Via Post Office, PC World, January 16, 2001.

- NetPost Mailing Online
  www.usps.gov/mailingonline/
- Federal Files Go Digital Via Post Office
  www.pcworld.com/news/article.asp?aid=38763

No Need for Acrobat-ics: 3 New Ways to Create PDF Files, ZDNet, October 19, 2001 describes three inexpensive shareware tools for creating PDF files and converting documents into PDF.

- No Need for Acrobat-ics: 3 New Ways to Create PDF Files
  www.zdnet.com/anchordesk/stories/story/0,10738,2818436,00.html

Palm Computing for Legal Professionals, LLRX, August 1, 2001. Legal technology expert Dennis Kennedy discusses the advantages of using Palm Pilots for lawyers. He also includes a list of tips for making the best use of them.

- Palm Computing for Legal Professionals
  www.llrx.com/features/pda3.htm

PCPitstop, in association with PC World, offers a free self-diagnostic test to measure your computer's efficiency. It also provides articles and links about services and products for improving computer performance.

- PCPitstop
  www.pcpitstop.com/

Speaking Naturally to Our Computers, Law Office Technology Review, October 1, 2001 is a survey of speech recognition software products for the law office.

- Speaking Naturally to Our Computers
www.law.com/cgi-bin/gx.cgi/AppLogic+FTContentServer?pagename=law/View&c=Article&cid=ZZZWIMZV0SC&live=true&cst=6&pc=0&pa=0&s=News&ExpIgnore=true&showsummary=0

Start With a Scanner, Law Technology News, October 15, 2001 is an overview of document conversion and its benefits for organizing office files and protecting against disaster.

- Start With a Scanner
www.law.com/cgi-bin/gx.cgi/AppLogic+FTContentServer?pagename=law/View&c=Article&cid=ZZZ8USLPNSC&live=true&cst=6&pc=0&pa=0&s=News&ExpIgnore=true&showsummary=0

TechSoup is nonprofit technology assistance organization whose mission is to provide information and resources for nonprofit organizations. The site contains links to discounted software and hardware products, information on training, consulting, funding and many other usefully topics.

- TechSoup
techsoup.org/

What to Do With a Problem Computer (Consumer Reports 2001) is an online resource guide for computer users. It provides advice, strategy, information, and tools for evaluating and fixing computer problems.

- What to Do With a Problem Computer
www.consumerreports.org/main/detail.jsp?CONTENT%3C%3Ecnt_id=84767&FOLDER%3C%3Efolder_id=84747&bmUID=1009395526200

LEGAL RESEARCH

Adventures of an On-Line Litigator, Erie County Bar Bulletin, June 2000. Written by Glenn Edward Murray, author of Collateral Consequences of Criminal Conduct (NYSBA), this article identifies on-line sources used by the author in recent cases that show the value of Internet resources and e-mail. This article illustrates practical uses in criminal and civil litigation.

- Adventures of an On-Line Litigator
www.eriebar.org/bulletin/june_2000/adventures.html
- Glenn Edward Murray
buffalo.usalawnet.com/profiles/02135_pp.htm
- Collateral Consequences of Criminal Conduct
www.nysba.org/cle/clepublications/crimconduct.html

ALWD Citation Manual (Association of Legal Writing Directors 2001) is a new entry into the legal citation guide arena. Touted as a rival to The Bluebook, it relies on one citation style for all documents. The book is in use in nearly 100 law schools.

- ALWD Citation Manual
www.alwd.org/cm/index.htm

California Criminal Law. Boalt Hall School of Law has launched a new full-text web enabled periodical into the small pool of law reviews concerning criminal law. Its inaugural issue contains the following articles of interest: Using International Law to Defend the Accused and Mental Illness and the Death Penalty.

- California Criminal Law
www.boalt.org/CCLR/
- Using International Law to Defend the Accused
www.boalt.org/CCLR/v1/v1amannfr.htm
- Mental Illness and the Death Penalty
www.boalt.org/CCLR/v1/v1sloboginfr.htm

Electronic Advance Sheets from Lexis-Nexis are email summaries of recent cases based on topic area or jurisdiction (i.e., specific state or federal court). Each decision includes the case summary found in Lexis opinions online with a hyperlink to the full-text of the decision. There is a subscription fee.

- Electronic Advance Sheets www.lexisone.com/advancesheets/advsubscribe?action=Continue&NextPage=ASHomePage
- Lexis-Nexis www.lexis.com

Findlaw Newsletters are free email summaries of new court opinions from the United States Supreme Court, federal circuit courts and state courts, such as New York, California, Texas and Florida. Findlaw recently added legal documents in the news to the list, which are complaints and motions filed in notable cases. Case summaries are sent to subscribers by email and are grouped by subject area or jurisdiction.

- Findlaw Newsletters newsletters.findlaw.com
- Findlaw www.findlaw.com

First Gov (Office of FirstGov 2001) is intended to cut government red tape and provide "rapid access to government information and services to the public."

- First Gov www.firstgov.com/

Lawyer's Guide to Internet Research, by Kathy Biehl, a columnist for LLRX.com and The Internet Legal Research Newsletter, and Tara Calishain, editor of ResearchBuzz, "is a pioneering book that leads lawyers, paralegals, legal assistants, and students through the transition from traditional to Internet research, and teaches them how to use the Internet to do the same work that they have been doing for years in their offices and libraries."

- Lawyer's Guide to Internet Research www.scarecrowpress.co

- m/Catalog/SingleBook.shtml?command=Search&db=^DB/CATALOG.db&eqSKUdata=0810838850
- LLRX.com
  www.llrx.com/
- The Internet Legal Research Newsletter
  www.netforlawyers.com/legal_research_news_archive.htm
- ResearchBuzz
  www.researchbuzz.com/

Legal Dictionaries is a segment of Lexis-Nexis' free Legal Internet Guide that contains an annotated list of a various legal lexicons available for free. They range widely from dictionaries on international law or divorce to the classic <u>Bouvier's Law Dictionary</u> (1856).

- Legal Dictionaries
  www.lexisone.com/legalresearch/legalguide/desk_references/legal_dictionaries.htm

Legal Information Buyer's Guide and Reference Manual 2001 (Rhode Island Law Press) is an authoritative guide to legal resources containing thorough descriptions, price information and cost saving tips. It is a valuable guide to lawyers interested in improving or expanding their law libraries.

- Legal Information Buyer's Guide and Reference Manual 2001
  rilawpress.com/

Lexis Pay as You Go is a customized legal research option offered by Lexis-Nexis to help lawyers economize in doing online research. Different packages are available in which the user can choose to pay for access, document retrieval or shepardizing for a day, a week or a month.

- Lexis Pay as You Go
  www.lexisone.com/specialoffer/getOffer?action=main

LexisONE is a legal database that is new, current and free. Lexis has created a national database of case law that contains decisions from 1996 to the present. A rich library of forms and an annotated legal research guide are also available. Read more about it in LexisONE: The New Internet Resource for Small Firm Attorneys and Solos LLRX, July 6, 2000.

- LexisONE
  www.lexisone.com/
- LexisONE: The New Internet Resource for Small Firm Attorneys and Solos
  www.llrx.com/extras/lexisone.htm

Locating the Law (4th ed. 2001) is a legal research guide produced by the Southern California Association of Law Libraries that covers the fundamentals of federal and state (California) law. It contains chapters on citation interpretation, research and collection development. This is a valuable guide for librarians and laypersons.

- Locating the Law
  www.aallnet.org/chapter/scall/locatingthelaw.html

Martindale-Hubbell's Law Digest Online is the web version of the law digest that accompanies the printed volumes of their directory. It contains digests of laws from all the states and 80 countries. Access is free.

- Martindale-Hubbell's Law Digest Online
  corporate.martindale.com/xp/Corporate/Login/introduction.xml

My Findlaw. Users can customize the vast amount of materials available from Findlaw, including legal news, federal and state case law, legal job listings, message boards and other invaluable web resources, saving them time as they use the Internet for legal research and business.

- My Findlaw
  my.findlaw.com/
- Findlaw
  www.findlaw.com

Preview of VersusLaw's USConline, CFRonline, and CFRupdate!, LLRX, September 17, 2001 describes the latest addition to the VersusLaw database. Known for its inexpensive collection of appellate court decisions, VersusLaw is incorporating the United States Code and the Code of Federal Regulations. An update service for the CFR is also being added. The pricing scheme for these new databases will be consistent with VersusLaw's policy of providing low-cost access to legal research.

- Preview of VersusLaw's USConline, CFRonline, and CFRupdate! www.llrx.com/features/cfrusc.htm

Real Life Dictionary of the Law is a new service provided by Law.com. It is an online dictionary of basic legal terms. It can be searched using the exact term or any term appearing in a definition. Unlike other legal dictionaries, it is not overwhelmed by numerous citations to cases and statutes. It is a resource for lay people or to help clients understand basic concepts.

- Real Life Dictionary of the Law dictionary.law.com/
- Law.com www.law.com

Survey of Online Legal Information Alternatives for Small Law Firms and Public Law Libraries, LLRX, November 1, 2001 is a review and comparison of free and low cost web-based legal research databases.

- Survey of Online Legal Information Alternatives for Small Law Firms and Public Law Libraries www.llrx.com/features/alternatives.htm

Update to a Guide to the U.S. Federal Legal System: Web-Based Publicly Accessible Sources, LLRX, November 1, 2001 is a comprehensive guide to federal legal resources on the web including links to research tutorials.

- Update to a Guide to the U.S. Federal Legal System: Web-Based Publicly Accessible Sources www.llrx.com/features/us_fed.htm

Weighing the Benefits of Legal Portals LLRX, December 17, 2001 reviews large and small legal research web portals, i.e., comprehensive collections of resources.

- Weighing the Benefits of Legal Portals
www.llrx.com/columns/notes48.htm

LEGAL SERVICES

Educating the Public About the Law (ABA 2001), published by the ABA Division for Public Education, is a booklet that presents an overview of how lawyers and judges can help public education programs, complete with tips, resources, sample programs and personal stories. The Public Education Division also published online a list of resources about the Right to Counsel and Legal Services for the Poor.

- Educating the Public About the Law
www.abanet.org/publiced/educatingpublicprint1.pdf
- Right to Counsel and Legal Services for the Poor
www.abanet.org/publiced/resources/right_to_counsel.html

Federal Poverty Guidelines 2001 are published each year in the Federal Register by the Department of Health and Human Services. The guidelines are the poverty thresholds for determining financial eligibility for certain federal programs and public defense representation.

- Federal Poverty Guidelines 2001
aspe.hhs.gov/poverty/01poverty.htm

Helping.org is a one-stop online resource designed to help people find volunteer and giving opportunities in their own communities and beyond. Moreover, it contains resources for non-profit organizations developing web sites, using the web for communication, advocacy or fund raising and ideas for obtaining funds for acquiring technology.

- Helping.org
  www.helping.org/

Homelessness: Programs and the People They Serve (Urban Institute 1999). This is a report on the results of a national survey concerning the homeless and their service providers.

- Homelessness: Programs and the People They Serve
  www.abanet.org/crimjust/pubs/reports/

New York State Bar Association Committee on Attorneys in Public Service web site provides information and resources for government and public sector attorneys, including the publication of the Government, Law and Public Policy Journal.

- New York State Bar Association Committee on Attorneys in Public Service
  www.nysba.org/committees/aps/default.htm
- Government, Law and Public Policy Journal
  www.nysba.org/committees/aps/publications.htm

Pro Bono Opportunities Guide: A Guide for Lawyers Outside of New York City (NYSBA 2nd ed. 2001) and **Pro Bono Opportunities: A Guide for Lawyers in New York City** (NYSBA 1999) are two comprehensive annotated guides to state and local pro bono programs. For more information about New York pro bono programs, visit the NYSBA Pro Bono Affairs web site.

- Pro Bono Opportunities Guide: A Guide for Lawyers Outside of New York City
  www.nysba.org/public/probono/Guide.pdf
- Pro Bono Opportunities: A Guide for Lawyers in New York City
  www.abcny.org/probabt.htm

- NYSBA Pro Bono Affairs
www.nysba.org/public/probono/probono.html

SPAN Report: Access to Justice Partnerships, State by State (NLADA 2001) describes the status of Access to Justice structures and initiatives nationwide. Supporting Partnerships to Expand Access to Justice (SPAN) is a joint project of the American Bar Association and the National Legal Aid and Defender Association, whose mission is to promote and support state-based partnerships among the bar, the courts, and legal services providers to expand access to justice.

- SPAN Report: Access to Justice Partnerships, State by State
www.nlada.org/Civil/Civil_SPAN/SPAN_Report

Using Tech Tools to Serve the Underserved, LexisONE, December 21, 2001 describes the impact that the Internet is having on pro bono services and making connections between clients and attorneys.

- Using Tech Tools to Serve the Underserved
www.lexisone.com/practicemanagement/pmlibrary/pm121201b.html

LITIGATION

2001 National Seminar for Public Defenders is nearly 1000 pages of training materials on a wide spectrum of topics for federal defenders. The materials were published in conjunction with the Advanced Seminar for CJA Panel Attorneys by the Administrative Office of the United States Courts. Additional federal public defender training materials are available online from the Federal Public Defender for the District of Columbia.

- 2001 National Seminar for Public Defenders
www.dcfpd.org/2001seminar/2001%20New%20Approaches.pdf
- Federal Public Defender for the District of Columbia

www.dcfpd.org/training
material.htm

Biased Interpretation of Evidence by Mock Jurors
Journal of Experimental Psychology: Applied, June 2001. This study examines the effect that new evidence has on the incipient opinions formed in the minds of jurors in the early stages of a trial.

- Biased Interpretation of Evidence by Mock Jurors
www.apa.org/journals/xap/xap7291.html

Effective Use of Courtroom Technology: A Judge's Guide to Pretrial and Trial (FJC/NITA 2001). This publication describes the substantive and procedural considerations that arise when lawyers use electronic equipment in the courtroom for presenting demonstrative evidence. Read more about these developments in courtroom technology in Computers and the Changing Courtroom, Legal Times, October 15, 2001.

- Effective Use of Courtroom Technology: A Judge's Guide to Pretrial and Trial
www.fjc.gov/public/pdf.nsf/lookup/CTtech00.pdf/$file/CTtech00.pdf
- Computers and the Changing Courtroom
www.law.com/cgi-bin/gx.cgi/AppLogic+FTContentServer?pagename=law/View&c=Article&cid=ZZZWZOMJMSC&live=true&cst=6&pc=0&pa=0&s=News&ExpIgnore=true&showsummary=0

How to Outsource Your Trial Support, Law Technology News, December 3, 2001 describes the pros and cons of hiring and working with an outside litigation support vendor to handle large cases.

- How to Outsource Your Trial Support
www.law.com/cgi-bin/gx.cgi/AppLogic+FTContentServer?pagename=law/View&c=Article&cid=ZZZMLBJLLUC&live=true&cst=6&pc=0&pa

=0&s=News&ExpIgnore
=true&showsummary=0

Pretrial Services Resource Center "is an independent, non-profit clearinghouse for information on pretrial issues and a technical assistance provider for pretrial practitioners, criminal justice officials, academicians, and community leaders nationwide. The Center offers assistance regarding pretrial services programming and management, and jail overcrowding."

- Pretrial Services Resource Center www.pretrial.org/

State of the Art: Computers in Litigation, Legal Times, October 29, 2001 discusses various computer applications for handling case information in court such as electronic document management and case analysis software.

- State of the Art: Computers in Litigation www.law.com/cgi-bin/gx.cgi/AppLogic+FT

ContentServer?pagename=law/View&c=Article&cid=ZZZIYMVY7TC&live=true&cst=6&pc=0&pa=0&s=News&ExpIgnore=true&showsummary=0

Use of Computer-Generated Exhibits in Federal Criminal Cases (Federal Public Defender for the District of Columbia 2001) is an overview of the use and admissibility under the Federal Rules of Evidence of computer-generated demonstrative and substantive evidence. It also discusses challenges and various situations related to its use in court.

- Use of Computer-Generated Exhibits in Federal Criminal Cases www.dcfpd.org/library/Comp.%20Gen.%20Exhibits.pdf

LOCATING INMATES
Federal Inmate Locator (BOP 2001) is a new service from the Federal Bureau of Prisons that enables web users to find information about someone in federal detention from 1982 to the

present. In addition to identification data, the site provides age, race, gender and release dates. There are links to the federal prison directory, visiting hours and descriptions of prison services. A national map of federal facilities is also available.

- Federal Inmate Locator www.bop.gov/inmate.html
- Federal Bureau of Prisons www.bop.gov/
- National Map of Federal Facilities www.dcfpd.org/library/bop_map.htm

LOCATING LAWYERS

Find a Lawyer (Findlaw 2001) is a new attorney directory provided by Findlaw with over 500,000 listings. In addition, it contains links to articles, consumer information and other useful sites.

- Find a Lawyer directory.findlaw.com/
- Findlaw www.findlaw.com

Finding Lawyers: Directories, Web Sites and State Bar Sources, LLRX, December 17, 2001 is a review of public and private attorney directories and includes a listing of online sources arranged by state.

- Finding Lawyers: Directories, Web Sites and State Bar Sources www.llrx.com/columns/reference32.htm

National Directory of Minority Attorneys (American Lawyer Media 2000). This specialized directory of attorneys was compiled by the Minority Law Journal and it can be searched by state and various topical groupings.

- National Directory of Minority Attorneys www.minoritylawjournal.com/directory/
- Minority Law Journal www.minoritylawjournal.com

LOCATING PUBLIC OFFICIALS

AOL's My Government Page can locate a variety of information about federal and state elected representatives based on zip code, including photographs, voting records and email addresses.

- AOL's My Government Page
government.aol.com/my news/

C-Span Congressional Directory is a tool for locating information about members of Congress, legislative committees and the leadership. Contact information for legislators and staffers can be found through a variety of searches, e.g., alphabetically, by state or zip code. It is a comprehensive and valuable resource for background research on federal legislators.

- C-Span Congressional Directory
congress.nw.dc.us/c-span/congdir.html

New Member Pictorial Directory 107th Congress (GPO 2000). Background information and pictures of the newest members of Congress are available in PDF format from the U.S. Government Printing Office's web site.

- New Member Pictorial Directory 107th Congress
www.gpo.gov/congress/107numem/index.html

Uncle Sam Who's Who in the Federal Government, which is maintained by the Government Publications Department at the University of Memphis, provides up-to-date biographical information on leading figures in the federal government.

- Uncle Sam Who's Who in the Federal Government

www.lib.memphis.edu/gpo/whos3.htm

United States Government Manual 2001/2002 (GPO) is the official handbook of the federal government. The entire manual is online. However,

- United States Government Manual 2001/2002
www.access.gpo.gov/nara/browse-gm-01.html

MEDICAL INFORMATION

Free Medical Journals is a comprehensive site containing links and information about medical journals online. The journals cover a wide range of subjects, and are sorted by topic.

- Free Medical Journals
www.freemedicaljournals.com/

Health on the Net Foundation is a search engine that accesses medical web sites and databases.

- Health on the Net Foundation
www.hon.ch/

Lab Tests Online (American Association for Clinical Chemistry 2001) is an encyclopedic resource for interpreting and understanding the results of medical tests and lab reports. Search engines locate information by type of test, medical condition or screening. It was created by a group of professional societies to better improve consumer understanding of medical testing.

- Lab Tests Online
www.labtestsonline.org/

Merck Manual of Diagnosis and Therapy (17th ed. 2000). "First published in 1899, The Merck Manual is the oldest continuously published general medical textbook in the English language and the most widely used medical textbook in the world. It covers almost every disease that affects humans in specialties such as pediatrics, obstetrics and gynecology, psychiatry, ophthalmology, otolaryngology, dermatology, and dentistry, and special situations such as burns, heat disorders, radiation reactions and injuries, and sports injuries." Available online in text and interactive formats.

- Merck Manual of Diagnosis and Therapy www.merckhomeedition.com/

Pharma-Lexicon: A Dictionary of Pharmaceutical Medicine is a web-based medical dictionary that contains search engines for finding the meanings of acronyms, abbreviations and drug information. It also includes links to medical related resources, news and research sites. The site can be viewed in English or Spanish.

- Pharma-Lexicon: A Dictionary of Pharmaceutical Medicine www.pharma-lexicon.com/

Researching Medical Literature on the Internet—2001 Update, LLRX, September 3, 2001 is a comprehensive study of medical research databases and web-based resources.

- Researching Medical Literature on the Internet -- 2001 Update www.llrx.com/features/medical2001.htm

SUMSearch looks for medical information by searching multiple Internet sites and collating the results into one page. The search can be tailored in a number of ways and lists of search terms are available.

- SUMSearch sumsearch.uthscsa.edu/searchform4.htm

MENTAL ILLNESS

Mental Health and Treatment of Inmates and Probationers (BJS 1999) is a survey of mentally ill offenders in prison, jail or on probation and describes treatment received while in custody.

- Mental Health and Treatment of Inmates and Probationers www.ojp.usdoj.gov/bjs/abstract/mhtip.htm

Mental Health Treatment in State Prisons, 2000 (BJS 2001). "Reports on facility policies related to screening of inmates at intake, conducting psychiatric or psychological evaluations, and providing treatment (including 24-hour mental health care, therapy/counseling, and use of psychotropic medications) in State prisons."

- Mental Health Treatment in State Prisons, 2000
www.ojp.usdoj.gov/bjs/abstract/mhtsp00.htm

NEW YORK COURTS
City, Town and Village Courts Resource Center

(OCA 2001). The Center offers research services for New York State's City, Town and Village Judges and court personnel. While access to the site is limited to judges and court personnel, there are research links to related associations with valuable information, such as the Mandatory Surcharge Schedule—Town and Village Courts.

- City, Town and Village Courts Resource Center www.courts.state.ny.us/oca/resourcecenter/
- Mandatory Surcharge Schedule—Town and Village Courts www.nymagistrate.com/nysmcca/news.htm

Community Outreach and Education Web Site

(OCA 2001). The Office of Court Administration has created a web site containing a well-organized collection of consumer information about New York Courts. It includes links to educational tools, court user guides, OCA publications and other court related resources from various agencies.

- Community Outreach and Education Web Site www.courts.state.ny.us/Community Outreach/
- New York Office of Court Administration www.courts.state.ny.us/

Court Rules and Individual Judges' Rules for the New York State and Federal Courts

(NYLJ) Comprehensive collection of court rules for

New York and Federal judges.

- Court Rules and Individual Judges' Rules for the New York State and Federal Courts www4.law.com/ny/rules/index.shtml

Courts of New York (NYSBA). An updated version of the New York State Bar Association's guide, Courts of New York, has been published in print and is also available on the web. It contains an outline of the court system and definitions of various legal terms aimed at enlightening the general public about the operation of the justice system in New York.

- Courts of New York www.nysba.org/public/courts.html
- New York State Bar Association www.nysba.org

E-Court (OCA 2001). New York's Office of Court Administration has launched a new service that permits users to search the civil and criminal dockets of courts in 30 counties and access decisions from courts in select counties.

- E-Court e.courts.state.ny.us/
- New York Office of Court Administration www.courts.state.ny.us/

New York Slip Opinion Service published by the New York Law Reporting Bureau, has expanded its database of New York appellate court slip opinions. The most recently released decisions are posted on their web site and remain there for 60 days. "The Court of Appeals has authorized a pilot program under which trial court and Appellate Term decisions not selected for publication in the Miscellaneous Reports may be published in the Slip Opinion Service." Browsing by date and field searching is available.

- New York Slip Opinion Service www.courts.state.ny.us/r

Insider's Guide to Criminal Justice Resources

- eporter/New_Features.htm
- Research the Official Reports
  www.courts.state.ny.us/reporter/Decisions.htm
- New York State Law Reporting Bureau
  www.courts.state.ny.us/reporter/

New York State Commission on Judicial Conduct 2001 Annual Report. "The Commission's annual reports contain informative descriptions of the year's [2000] activities, including statistics and accounts of investigations, disciplinary actions, confidential cautions and other dispositions. Also included are legislative and administrative recommendations, commentary on selected topics, texts of disciplinary determinations, and more."

- New York State Commission on Judicial Conduct 2001 Annual Report
  www.scjc.state.ny.us/annual.html

New York State Law Reporting Bureau (2000). This site offers information about the Bureau's operations and publications. It also contains the Official Reports Style Manual and links to the New York Slip Opinion Service.

- New York State Law Reporting Bureau
  www.courts.state.ny.us/reporter/
- Official Reports Style Manual
  www.courts.state.ny.us/reporter/Styman.htm
- New York Slip Opinion Service
  www.courts.state.ny.us/reporter/Decisions.htm

New York State Unified Court System Library and Information Network (OCA 2001). Access to a combined catalog of New York court libraries, known as LION, has been made available by the Office of Court Administration. In addition, indices to Appellate Division Records and Briefs can be searched.

- New York State Unified Court System Library and Information Network
www.courts.state.ny.us/LION/index.html
- New York Office of Court Administration
www.courts.state.ny.us/

New York's Appellate Division <u>Third Department</u> and <u>Fourth Department</u> have launched web sites providing access to recent decisions. The sites include basic court information, calendars, court rules and information about other services of interest to practitioners and the general public.

- Third Department
www.courts.state.ny.us/ad3/
- Fourth Department
www.courts.state.ny.us/ad4/

POLICE MISCONDUCT

Cruelty in Control? The Stun Belt and Other Electroshock Weapons in Law Enforcement (AI 1999) is a report about the consequences of law enforcement's use of chemical and stun weapons, i.e., less than lethal weapons, to subdue suspects.

- Cruelty in Control? The Stun Belt and Other Electroshock Weapons in Law Enforcement
www.amnestyusa.org/rightsforall/stun/index.html

Disciplining Police: Solving the Problem of Law Enforcement (New York City Public Advocate 2000). The Public Advocate's Office conducted a study of the system for disciplining police officers in New York City. The report explores the police department's response to complaints of misconduct, the possible factors behind such behavior and makes policy recommendations based on its findings.

- Disciplining Police: Solving the Problem of Law Enforcement
www.pubadvocate.nyc.gov/documents/polfinalo72700.pdf

Principles for Promoting Police Integrity

(BJA 2001) "We have sought to identify and develop general principles of police practices that are effective in promoting police integrity. We hope that by sharing what we have learned, we can build on the voluntary efforts being made by police departments around the country to improve their services, and more clearly state what communities can expect of us as law enforcement agencies."

- Principles for Promoting Police Integrity
  www.ncjrs.org/pdffiles1/ojp/186189.pdf

Race, Rights and Police Brutality in the United States of America

(AI 1999) is a report about brutality and racism in policing and makes recommendations for reform.

- Race, Rights and Police Brutality in the United States of America
  www.amnestyusa.org/rights forall/police/index.html

Shielded from Justice: Police Brutality and Accountability in the United States

(HRW 1998) is a study of issues concerning police accountability over the use of excessive force and other abuses. It focuses on brutality cases that occurred in fourteen cities over a two-year period.

- Shielded from Justice: Police Brutality and Accountability in the United States
  www.hrw.org/reports98/police/index.htm

U.S. Department of State Initial Report of the United States of America to the UN Committee Against Torture

(DOS 1999) is a report describing the measures taken by the U.S. Government to comply with the guidelines in the Convention Against Torture, and Other Cruel, Inhuman, or Degrading Treatment or Punishment.

- U.S. Department of State Initial Report of the United States of America to the UN Committee Against Torture
www.state.gov/www/global/human_rights/torture_index.html
- Convention Against Torture, and Other Cruel, Inhuman, or Degrading Treatment or Punishment
www.unhchr.ch/html/menu3/b/h_cat39.htm

Use of Deadly Force by Police: Overview of National and Local Data (NIJ 1999) is an overview of research about police use of deadly force at different levels and from different perspectives.

- Use of Deadly Force by Police: Overview of National and Local Data
www.ojp.usdoj.gov/bjs/abstract/ufbponld.htm

POST-CONVICTION

Federal Habeas Corpus Review and **The New Habeas Corpus Act: A Checklist for Practitioners** are part of the Findlaw for Legal Professionals section containing analyses of current developments in different areas of law.

- Federal Habeas Corpus Review
profs.lp.findlaw.com/habeas/index.html
- The New Habeas Corpus Act: A Checklist for Practitioners
profs.lp.findlaw.com/habeas/checklist.html
- Findlaw for Legal Professionals
profs.lp.findlaw.com/

Postconviction DNA Testing: Recommendations for Handling Requests (National Commission on the Future of DNA Evidence 1999)

- Postconviction DNA Testing: Recommendations for Handling Requests
www.ncjrs.org/pdffiles1/nij/177626.pdf

Presidential Pardons is a new collection of resources from JURIST: The Legal

Education Network at the University of Pittsburgh School of Law that contains news, case law, bibliographies and many other resources for anyone interested in executive clemency.

- Presidential Pardons jurist.law.pitt.edu/pardons.htm
- JURIST: The Legal Education Network jurist.law.pitt.edu/index.htm

PRISON STATISTICS

Census of Jails 1999 (BJS 2001). "The report summarizes changes in the number of local jails during the 1990's; average daily population and number of men, women, and juveniles confined in local jails; number of inmates and facilities by size of facility; inmate conviction status; inmate gender, race and Hispanic origin; facility rated capacity and percent of capacity occupied; 25 largest jail jurisdictions; number of staff and staff characteristics; facility health services and inmate health; and facility programs."

- Census of Jails 1999 www.ojp.usdoj.gov/bjs/abstract/cj99.htm

Correctional Trends (BJS 2001) is a graphical summary of incarceration rates, prison population trends, including death penalty statistics.

- Correctional Trends www.ojp.usdoj.gov/bjs/glance.htm

Corrections Statistics (BJS 2000) is a report on the increase in the number of people in prison, on probation or parole in the United States.

- Corrections Statistics www.ojp.usdoj.gov/bjs/correct.htm

HIV in Prisons and Jails, 1999 (BJS 2001). "Provides the number of HIV-positive and active AIDS cases among prisoners held in each State and the Federal prison system at yearend 1999."

- HIV in Prisons and Jails, 1999

www.ojp.usdoj.gov/bjs/pub/pdf/hivpj99.pdf

Prison and Jail Inmates at Midyear 2000 (BJS 2001). "Presents data on prison and jail inmates collected from National Prisoner Statistics counts and the Annual Survey of Jails in 2000. This report provides data on the number of inmates, the total incarceration rate per 100,000 residents in each State, and the trends since 1990. It offers percentage changes in the size of State and Federal prison populations since the end of 1999 and midyear 1999. The report includes total numbers for prison and jail inmates by gender, race, and Hispanic origin as well as counts of jail inmates by juvenile status, conviction status, and confinement status. The midyear report also presents findings on rated capacity of local jails, percent of capacity occupied, and capacity added."

- Prison and Jail Inmates at Midyear 2000

www.ojp.usdoj.gov/bjs/abstract/pjim00.htm

Prisoner Petitions Filed in U.S. District Courts, 2000, With Trends, 1980-2000 (BJS 2001). This report describes the number of prisoner petitions filed by Federal and State inmates in U.S. district courts during the year 2000. It estimates the impact of the Prison Litigation Reform Act and the Antiterrorism and Effective Death Penalty Act on the number of prisoner petitions.

- Prisoner Petitions Filed in U.S. District Courts, 2000, With Trends, 1980-2000
www.ojp.usdoj.gov/bjs/abstract/ppfusd00.htm

Prisoners in 2000 (BJS 2001). This report describes the number of persons in state and federal prisons and compares the increase in prison population during 2000 with that of the previous year, along with the growth rates since 1990.

- Prisoners in 2000
  www.ojp.usdoj.gov/bjs/abstract/p00.htm

Prisoners in 1999 (BJS 2000). This report reveals a startling rise in America's prison population over the last ten years.

- Prisoners in 1999
  www.ojp.usdoj.gov/bjs/abstract/ppfusd00.htm

Probation and Parole in the United States, 2000 (BJS 2001). "Reports on the number of persons on probation and parole at yearend 2000 and compares the totals with yearend 1999 and 1990. It lists the number of parolees and probationers in each State, names the States with the largest and smallest parole and probation populations and the largest and smallest rates of community supervision, and identifies the States with the biggest increases."

- Probation and Parole in the United States, 2000
  www.ojp.usdoj.gov/bjs/abstract/ppus00.htm

Punishing Decade: Prison and Jail Estimates at the Millennium (Justice Policy Institute 1999) is a report about the record high numbers of people in American prisons and the implications of an increasing prison population.

- Punishing Decade: Prison and Jail Estimates at the Millennium
  www.cjcj.org/punishingdecade/punishing.html

Trends in State Parole, 1990-2000 (BJS 2001) examines the changing nature of offenders entering and leaving parole and the effects on the trends and composition of the prison population.

- Trends in State Parole, 1990-2000
  www.ojp.usdoj.gov/bjs/abstract/tsp00.htm

PRISONERS' RIGHTS
Abuse of Women in Custody: Sexual Misconduct and Shackling of Pregnant Women: A State-by-State Survey of Policies and Practices in the

United States (AI 2001) "The information compiled in this report, based on a survey by Amnesty International, summarizes existing legislation, policies and practices in every state, the District of Columbia and the US Bureau of Prisons and reviews these areas in the context of international human rights standards. The main concerns arising from the surveys are the continuing lack of laws prohibiting custodial sexual misconduct in some states; the failure of existing laws to provide adequate protection; and the widespread lack of legislation and uniform standards, in policy and practice, to protect incarcerated women in labor from being shackled during child birth. Amnesty International believes legislative and policy shortcomings in these areas contribute to human rights abuses against inmates."

- Abuse of Women in Custody: Sexual Misconduct and Shackling of Pregnant Women: A State-by-State Survey of Policies and Practices in the United States
www.amnestyusa.org/women/custody/abuseincustody.html

Aging Behind Bars: "Three Strikes" Seven Years Later (Sentencing Project 2001). This report concludes that the "three strikes" law has not contributed to the reduction of crime in California to any significant extent.

- Aging Behind Bars: "Three Strikes" Seven Years Later
www.sentencingproject.org/news/3strikesnew.pdf

From Prison to Home: The Dimensions and Consequences of Prisoner Reentry (Urban Institute 2001). This report "examines all aspects of prisoner reentry—from preparation for release to post-prison supervision. It identifies and addresses the challenges facing many released prisoners, such as substance abuse, health problems, employment obstacles and housing shortages, as well as the impact of their return on their families and neighborhoods."

- From Prison to Home: The Dimensions and Consequences of Prisoner Reentry www.urban.org/pdfs/from_prison_to_home.pdf

Integration of the Human Rights of Women and the Gender Perspective: Violence Against Women (U.N. Commission on Human Rights 1999) is a report concerning violence against women in federal and state prisons.

- Integration of the Human Rights of Women and the Gender Perspective: Violence Against Women www.unhchr.ch/Huridoc da/Huridoca.nsf/TestFr ame/7560a6237c67bb11 8025674c004406e9?Op endocument

Jail Breaks: Economic Development Subsidies Given to Private Prisons (Institute on Taxation and Economic Policy 2001). "This study examines an overlooked aspect of the billion-dollar private prison industry: the extent to which it has been the recipient of economic development subsidies provided by local, state and federal governments."

- Jail Breaks: Economic Development Subsidies Given to Private Prisons www.goodjobsfirst.org/jbstudy.htm

Making More Effective Use of New York State's Prisons (Citizens Budget Commission 2000) "The general conclusion of this analysis is that the State of New York could save nearly $100 million annually by avoiding unnecessary and sometimes counterproductive imprisonment. . . . By reducing the length of incarceration for some prisoners and substituting alternative forms of punishment for the latter part of their sentence, New Yorkers could save millions while maintaining or improving their level of public safety."

- Making More Effective Use of New York State's Prisons
www.cbcny.org/DOCS52000.htm

"Not Part of My Sentence" Violations of the Human Rights of Women in Custody (AI 1999) is an examination of the abuse and mistreatment of women in American prisons.

- "Not Part of My Sentence" Violations of the Human Rights of Women in Custody
www.amnestyusa.org/rightsforall/women/index.html

Red Onion State Prison: Super-Maximum Security Confinement in Virginia (HRW 1999) is a report on the treatment of inmates at Virginia's super-maximum prison and allegations of human rights violations.

- Red Onion State Prison: Super-Maximum Security Confinement in Virginia
www.hrw.org/reports/1999/redonion/

Second Look at Alleviating Jail Crowding: A Systems Perspective (BJA 2000) "Jail crowding must be recognized as a local problem and solutions developed in accordance with the unique circumstances of individual communities. While new construction to increase the number of jail beds may be one component of a set of proposed solutions to the problem, this document emphasizes other activities that can help to ensure the effective use of existing bed space. This monograph provides information to help jurisdictions study case processing and plan system wide strategies. Emphasis is placed on the role that local criminal justice agencies can play, alone and with others, to determine the best use of jail space to prevent crime and maintain public safety."

- Second Look at Alleviating Jail Crowding: A Systems Perspective www.ncjrs.org/pdffiles1/bja/182507.pdf

What Future for "Public Safety" and "Restorative Justice" in Community Corrections? (NIJ 2001). "'Public safety' and 'restorative justice' are big ideas now making claims on the future of community corrections. They are appealing as strategic objectives for probation and parole agencies that are unable to generate fiscal and political support for the modest objectives of 'enforcing court orders,' 'meeting client needs,' and 'reducing recidivism.' When the two ideas are examined more closely, however, their futures seem uncertain. They have important features in common, but they conflict in ways which, left unresolved, could sap their strategic value; they face challenges to which they are unevenly suited; and each requires daunting transformations of the criminal justice system."

- What Future for "Public Safety" and "Restorative Justice" in Community Corrections? www.ncjrs.org/pdffiles1/nij/187773.pdf

PRISONS
Corrections Connection was designed for practitioners in the prison community providing news, legislative updates, research links and resources.

- Corrections Connection www.corrections.com/about.html

Prison Web Sites. Notable and infamous prisons from different countries can now be visited through their web sites. These include: Tower of London, Eastern State Penitentiary in Philadelphia, Lubyanka and Robben Island For more information read Web Sites Unlock the Doors of Famous Prisons, New York Times, March 15, 2001.

- Tower of London www.tower-of-london.com/

- Eastern State Penitentiary in Philadelphia www.libertynet.org/~estate/
- Lubyanka www.globalspy.com/lubyanka.htm
- Robben Island www.robben-island.org.za/
- Web Sites Unlock the Doors of Famous Prisons www.nytimes.com/2001/03/15/technology/15GRAB.html

PROBLEM SOLVING COURTS

Problem Solving Courts: A Brief Primer (CCI 2001). "This essay . . . traces the history of problem-solving courts, outlines a basic set of problem-solving principles and poses a set of questions that are worthy of further study as problem-solving courts move from experiment to institutionalization."

- Problem Solving Courts: A Brief Primer www.courtinnovation.org/pdf/prob_solv_courts.pdf

Reflections of Problem-Court Justices (NYSBA 2000). "During its annual judicial seminar at the end of 1999, the Unified Court System convened a roundtable of problem-solving judges to discuss how their courts operate and how they affect the roles that judges play inside and outside the courtroom."

- Reflections of Problem-Court Justices www.nysba.org/media/barjournal/june00/judicial.html

Ten Tenets of Fair and Effective Problem Solving Courts (ACCD 2001) "The following guidelines have been developed to increase both the fairness and the effectiveness of Problem Solving Courts, while addressing concerns regarding the defense role within them. They are based upon the research done in the drug court arena by pretrial services experts and others and the extensive collective expertise that defender chiefs have developed as a result of their experiences with the many different specialty courts across the country."

- Ten Tenets of Fair and Effective Problem Solving Courts
www.nysda.org/Defense_Services/Ten_Tenets-Final_Version.pdf

PROFESSIONAL RESPONSIBILITY

Association of Professional Responsibility Lawyers (APRL) is an independent national organization of lawyers concentrating in the fields of professional responsibility and legal ethics. APRL provides a national clearinghouse of information regarding recent developments and emerging issues in the areas of admission to practice law, professional ethics, disciplinary standards and procedures, and professional liability.

- Association of Professional Responsibility Lawyers
www.aprl.net/

Ethics 2000 - Commission on the Evaluation of the Rules of Professional Conduct (ABA 2000). The Commission work evaluating the ABA Model Rules is being posted on this web site along with the latest information and drafts of proposed changes.

- Ethics 2000 - Commission on the Evaluation of the Rules of Professional Conduct
www.abanet.org/cpr/ethics2k.html

New York Professional Responsibility Reporter. The New York Professional Responsibility Report publishes a monthly print newsletter that contains articles and reports on developments in areas of ethics and professional responsibility with a focus on New York practice. Subscription information is available on their web site.

- New York Professional Responsibility Reporter
www.nyprr.com/

Restatement of the Law Governing Lawyers is the first edition by the American Law Institute (ALI) of a Restatement on ethics that clarifies and synthesizes the common law applicable to the legal profession.

- Restatement of the Law Governing Lawyers www.ali.org/ali/A252.htm
- American Law Institute www.ali.org/

Safety in Numbers: Revisiting the Risks to Client Confidences and Attorney-Client Privilege Posed by Internet Electronic Mail Berkley Technology Law Journal (Fall 1999). This article analyzes the preconceptions behind ethics opinions sanctioning attorney-client contact through email and points out methods for making those communications more secure.

- Safety in Numbers: Revisiting the Risks to Client Confidences and Attorney-Client Privilege Posed by Internet Electronic Mail www.law.berkeley.edu/journals/btlj/articles/14_3/Masur/html/reader.html

PUBLIC DEFENSE

Access to Justice Forum is an open discussion and database of resources on legal aid and access to justice world wide developed by the Public Interest Law Initiative in Transitional Societies at Columbia Law School.

- Access to Justice Forum www.pili.org/cgi-bin/a2j

Balancing Justice in New York State (LWVNY 2000) is a report by the League of Women Voters of New York, created after conducting statewide study circles on current criminal law issues. Among their findings, the majority of people recommended reforming the Rockefeller Drug Laws and most people see rehabilitation as one of the prime goals of the criminal justice system.

- Balancing Justice in New York State
www.lwvny.org/balancingjustice/finalreport.html

California Attorneys for Criminal Justice (CACJ) is the country's largest statewide organization of criminal defense lawyers and allied professionals. Their web site contains links to news about legislative developments, seminars and a list of useful publications for criminal practitioners.

- California Attorneys for Criminal Justice
www.cacj.org/

Compendium of Standards for Indigent Defense Systems (BJA 2000) "presents national, state, and local standards relating to five major aspects of indigent defense: Administration of Defense Systems (Volume I); Attorney Performance (Volume II); Capital Case Representation (Volume III); Appellate Representation (Volume IV); Juvenile Justice Defense (Volume V). These standards are non-case specific statements that help policymakers assess the adequacy or appropriateness of the provision of defense services to indigent defendants. Some standards are aspirational, that is, a goal for the future; other standards are enforced by operating or funding agencies. The standards and rules collected here were issued by national organizations; state agencies; bar associations, public defender agencies; state high courts; and local court or bar."

- Compendium of Standards for Indigent Defense Systems
www.ojp.usdoj.gov/indigentdefense/compendium

Contracting for Indigent Defense Services: A Special Report (Spangenberg—BJA 2000) "This special report was written for individuals in the justice system who are using, considering, or implementing an indigent defense contract system. The report presents the major judicial and legislative attempts to deal with those systems, examines the best and worst features of contract systems, and discusses the national standards that govern contract systems."

- Contracting for Indigent Defense Services: A Special Report www.ncjrs.org/pdffiles1/bja/181160.pdf

Defender Guidebook to Technology Integration in Criminal Justice Information Systems. The National Legal Aid and Defender Association (NLADA) has produced a "guidebook [that] discusses the components of integration, the top 10 defender interests in integration, and challenges and problems in areas such as planning, security, management, and human resources." It was produced for the Criminal Courts Technical Assistance Project at American University.

- Defender Guidebook to Technology Integration in Criminal Justice Information Systems www.american.edu/academ.depts/spa/justice/publications/TechGuide.pdf
- National Legal Aid and Defender Association www.nlada.org/
- Criminal Courts Technical Assistance Project www.american.edu/academ.depts/spa/justice/training.html

Defense Counsel in Criminal Cases (BJS 2000). "This Special Report examines issues of legal representation for defendants in Federal district court and large local jurisdictions, and inmates in local jails and Federal and State prison. It also briefly describes types of publicly financed programs available to both Federal and local defendants."

- Defense Counsel in Criminal Cases www.ojp.usdoj.gov/bjs/abstract/dccc.htm

Defense Warnings, American Bar Association Journal, December 2001 describes how overburdened public defenders seek redress by filing lawsuits over excessive caseloads and inadequate resources.

- Defense Warnings
  www.abanet.org/journal/dec01/fdefen.html

Executive Session on Public Defense (John F. Kennedy School of Government 2001) is a web site created after a meeting of public defenders and criminal justice experts who examined the public defense culture and developed strategies for improving public policy. The site contains an extensive collection of articles, studies, reports and resource links.

- Executive Session on Public Defense
  www.ksg.harvard.edu/criminaljustice/executive_sessions/espd.htm

Handbook for Criminal Defendants (OCA 2000). This Spanish language version of a guide to the New York Criminal Justice System is available online from the Office of Court Administration.

- Handbook for Criminal Defendants
  www.courts.state.ny.us/spcrimhand.html

How to Defend Someone You Know Is Guilty New York Times, April 8, 2001. David Feige, Trial Chief for The Bronx Defenders and a commentator for WNYC radio, offers a public defender's perspective on the vital role of criminal defense in a free society.

- How to Defend Someone You Know Is Guilty
  www.nytimes.com/2001/04/08/magazine/08GUILTY.html

Indigent Defense (BJS 1996). "This report presents selected findings drawn from various BJS surveys containing information related to the indigent defense for criminal defendants."

- Indigent Defense
  www.ojp.usdoj.gov/bjs/abstract/id.htm

Indigent Defense and Technology: A Progress Report (BJA 1999). This special report examines the changing role of technology in public defense offices and the ways it impacts on public defense practice. For more information, visit the Justice Information Center.

- Indigent Defense and Technology: A Progress Report www.ncjrs.org/pdffiles1/bja/179003.pdf
- Justice Information Center www.ncjrs.org/

Indigent Defense Services in Large Counties 1999 (BJS 2000). "This report details the methods by which criminal indigent defense is delivered in the Nation's 100 most populous counties. It compares the operating expenditures, staffing and caseload of public defender, assigned counsel, and contract services used in these counties. The criminal indigent defense programs examined in the report primarily handled felony criminal cases at the trial level."

- Indigent Defense Services in Large Counties 1999 www.ojp.usdoj.gov/bjs/abstract/idslc99.htm

Keeping Defender Workloads Manageable (BJA 2001). "[I]n some jurisdictions, public defender offices are appointed as many as 80 percent of all criminal cases." "The subject of this report, finding ways to better manage defender workloads, is at the heart of ensuring that the administration of justice is fair and equitable. Every day, defender offices and assigned counsel are forced to manage too many clients with inadequate resources. Too often, the quality of service suffers, jeopardizing one of our most important constitutional rights: the right to effective counsel."

- Keeping Defender Workloads Manageable www.ncjrs.org/pdffiles1/bja/185632.pdf

Public's Guide to the Courts

(OCA). The New York State Office of Court Administration has created an informational web guide for lay people seeking information about the legal system in New York. It includes links to a legal glossary, handbooks for defendants and jurors, and forms and directories.

- Public's Guide to the Courts www.courts.state.ny.us/pubinfo.htm
- Glossary of Legal Terms www.courts.state.ny.us/civilgloss.htm
- New York State Criminal Justice Handbook www.courts.state.ny.us/Handcrimdef.html
- Juror's Handbook www.courts.state.ny.us/juryhdbk.html
- New York State Office of Court Administration www.courts.state.ny.us

National Association of Criminal Defense Attorneys

(NACDL) has redesigned its web site to provide better access to its wealth of materials online, which include news, publications, developments in indigent defense and many other resources.

- National Association of Criminal Defense Attorneys www.criminaljustice.org

National Legal Aid and Defender Association

(NLADA) has redesigned its web site, which boasts many new features and resources. Public defense community members "can both obtain and directly contribute documents and current jobs and event information via the NLADA E-Library (a document database), the National Training Calendar, and the jobs and links listings."

- National Legal Aid and Defender Association www.nlada.org/

New Model Contract for Public Defense Services

(NLADA). The National Legal Aid and Defender Association "has published a Model Contract for Public

Defense Services, to help local funding agencies and indigent defense providers entering into a contracting relationship to identify and integrate the essential elements of high quality indigent defense services."

- New Model Contract for Public Defense Services www.nlada.org/indig/novdec99/modcon.htm
- National Legal Aid and Defender Association www.nlada.org/

New York Criminal Bar Association is a not-for-profit association for criminal defense lawyers in the New York City Metropolitan area. They have collected hundreds of telephone and fax numbers for judges, police precincts, arraignment clerks, correction officers and others in the criminal justice system.

- New York Criminal Bar Association www.nycrimbar.org/

New York State Defenders Association (NYSDA) has expanded its web site and improved access to its vast collection of current online resources. New Hot Topics have been added as well as unpublished decisions, briefs, reports, training calendar and a searchable expert database.

- New York State Defenders Association www.nysda.org

State-Funded Indigent Defense Services 1999 (BJS 2001). "Presents findings from data collected as part of the 1999 National Survey of Indigent Defense Systems in the 21 States where the State government provides virtually all of the funding for indigent defense services."

- State-Funded Indigent Defense Services 1999 www.ojp.usdoj.gov/bjs/abstract/sfids99.htm

Tutorial for Public Defender Managers (VIJ 2001). This is an online tutorial intended for public defenders "who want to enhance their leadership role in the criminal justice system, Vera's new web-based tutorial provides an introduction to strategic management, reflective practice, and asset-based management, and gives users a chance to compare their answers to anonymous defender managers who have taken the tutorial recently."

- Tutorial for Public Defender Managers
www.vera.org/tutorial/splash.asp

PUBLIC RECORDS

Access-Central is a large public records access portal. It has a collection of public records links, including people finders, licensing agencies and government databases nationwide. It also includes links to fee-based background checking and criminal history search services.

- Access-Central
www.access-central.com/

Accurint is a fee-based people tracking service that searches billions of records from hundreds of sources. It can locate people or unearth helpful background information.

- Accurint
www.accurint.com

Merlin Information Services is a collection of free and fee-based public record databases. "Merlin is one of the largest distributors of public records on CD-ROM in the nation." Their newest databases include Merlin's Date of Birth File, Public Record Research System, QuickInfo.net, Merlin Super Name Header Search and Merlin Super Address Header Search.

- Merlin Information Services
www.merlindata.com/

Public Records—Nationwide. Pacific Information Resources has made available a collection of links to government and private databases with information on prisoners, experts and county data for all fifty states and countries worldwide.

- Public Records—
  Nationwide
  www.pac-info.com/

PublicData.com is a fee-based public records search service. Its databases include criminal histories, sex offender registries, motor vehicle records and other sites. The scope of records available depends on the state. They offer a variety of subscription plans.

- PublicData.com
  www.publicdata.com/

RACE AND LAW

Attacking Bias in the Justice System: A Compendium of Program Alternatives (ABA Coalition for Justice 2000) is a collection of specific projects, programs and recommendations that bar associations, courts and communities can draw from to address bias in the justice system.

- Attacking Bias in the Justice System: A Compendium of Program Alternatives
  www.abanet.org/justice/judicialbias/home.html

Final Report of the [New Jersey] State Police Review Team (NJ Attorney General 1999). Reports and consent decrees regarding investigation into racial profiling in New Jersey have been compiled by the New Jersey Department of Law and Public Safety.

- Final Report of the [New Jersey] State Police Review Team
  www.state.nj.us/lps/Rpt ii.pdf
- New Jersey Department of Law and Public Safety
  www.state.nj.us/lps/decreehome.htm

Initial Report of the United States of America to the United Nations Committee on the Elimination of Racial Discrimination (Convention on the Elimination of All Forms of Racial Discrimination 2000). In this report, the U.S. Government described the legislative, judicial, administrative and other measures it has taken regarding the Convention on the Elimination of All Forms of Racial Discrimination.

- Initial Report of the United States of America to the United Nations Committee on the Elimination of Racial Discrimination state.gov/www/global/human_rights/cerd_report/cerd_index.html
- Convention on the Elimination of All Forms of Racial Discrimination www.unhchr.ch/html/menu3/b/d_icerd.htm

Justice on Trial: Racial Disparities in the American Criminal Justice System (Leadership Conference on Civil Rights 2000) describes the unequal treatment of minorities in the criminal justice system and reviews the impact of disparate treatment on the entire system.

- Justice on Trial: Racial Disparities in the American Criminal Justice System www.civilrights.org/publications/cj/

Off Balance: Youth, Race and Crime in the News (Building Blocks for Youth 2001). This study of crime news reporting revealed that "combined distortions of people of color overrepresented as criminals and underrepresented as victims, young people over-represented as criminals, and the undue coverage of violent crime, produce an inaccurate and unfair image of crime in America." It concluded with recommendations for the media to present crime news in context.

- Off Balance: Youth, Race and Crime in the News www.buildingblocksforyouth.org/media/media.html

Racial Profiling: Limited Data Available on Motorist Stops (GAO 2000) is a review of studies and data collection efforts by law enforcement agencies to measure racial profiling in traffic stops.

- Racial Profiling: Limited Data Available on Motorist Stops
www.gao.gov/new.items/gg00041.pdf

Resource Guide on Racial Profiling Data Collections Systems: Promising Practices and Lessons Learned (BJA 2000) "This document provides an overview of the nature of racial profiling; a description of data collection and its purpose; current activities in California, New Jersey, North Carolina, and Great Britain; and recommendations for the future."

- Resource Guide on Racial Profiling Data Collections Systems: Promising Practices and Lessons Learned
www.ncjrs.org/pdffiles1/bja/184768.pdf

Traffic Stop Data Collection Policies for State Police, 2001 (BJS 2001). "This report presents findings from the 2001 State Police Traffic Stop Data Collection Procedures. State police agencies were asked to report on their policies and procedures for collecting race and ethnicity data regarding motorists involved in traffic stops."

- Traffic Stop Data Collection Policies for State Police, 2001
www.ojp.usdoj.gov/bjs/abstract/tsdcp01.htm

REFERENCE TOOLS
Abbreviations and Acronyms of the U.S. Government, is a solid research tool that decrypts the code of federal lingo. It is part of a collection of Government Information Resources at the Indiana University Library.

- Abbreviations and Acronyms of the U.S. Government
www.ulib.iupui.edu/subjectareas/gov/docs_abbrev.html
- Government Information Resources

www.ulib.iupui.edu/subjectareas/gov/govdocs.html
- Indiana University Library www.ulib.iupui.edu/home.html

Almanacs is a search engine from the publishers of the Information Please Almanac. The site provides access to fact books, dictionaries, encyclopedias and other reference sources. It is a vast storehouse of useful factual knowledge.

- Almanacs www.infoplease.com/almanacs.html

American Heritage Dictionary of the English Language (4th ed. 2001). This online version of the Dictionary contains nearly a 100,000 entries along with language notes and other useful reference information.

- American Heritage Dictionary of the English Language www.bartleby.com/61/

AskOxford is a site intended to assist writers with questions about grammar, word usage and anything else related to the world of words. Among the many resources it provides is a panel of experts who answer questions on English usage. The site is sponsored by Oxford University Press, publishers of the Oxford English Dictionary.

- AskOxford www.askoxford.com/
- Oxford English Dictionary www.oed.com
- Oxford University Press www.oed.com/public/publications/online.htm

Associations on the Net published by the Internet Public Library, "is a collection of over 2000 Internet sites providing information about a wide variety of professional and trade associations, cultural and art organizations, political parties and advocacy groups, labor unions, academic societies, and research institutions. Abstracts summarizing information about the association and its site are provided."

- Associations on the Net www.ipl.org/ref/AON
- Internet Public Library www.ipl.org

CIA World Factbook 2001 is a reference tool for researching background information, statistics or maps for different countries. Prepared by the Central Intelligence Agency for use by U.S. Government officials it also contains a great deal of data about the political and organizational structure of the countries listed.

- CIA World Factbook 2001 www.odci.gov/cia/publications/factbook/index.html

Clickguide is a free web navigation tool that can be installed into your web browser. It contains menus for a vast number of services, including search engines, legal dictionaries and encyclopedias. A search box is generated for each web site, eliminating the need for bookmarks or hunting for reference tools on the web.

- Clickguide www.clickguide.com/upgrades/latest_version.htm

Columbia Encyclopedia (6th ed. 2001). This online edition of the Encyclopedia has nearly 51,000 entries on a broad range of topics. It can be browsed alphabetically or by keyword.

- Columbia Encyclopedia www.bartleby.com/65/

Country Watch contains current political, economic and cultural information about every country in the world.

- Country Watch www.countrywatch.com/default.asp

Journalist Express. This web site contains extensive links to news sources, phone directories, and statistics.

Insider's Guide to Criminal Justice Resources

- Journalist Express
  www.journalistexpress.com/

Oxford English Dictionary (Oxford University Press). The most comprehensive dictionary of the English language is available online. For information about subscribing, visit the publisher's site.

- Oxford English Dictionary
  www.oed.com/
- Oxford University Press
  www.oed.com/public/publications/online.htm

Phrase Finder is a writer's tool for generating ideas and finding the right word to express a particular thought.

- Phrase Finder
  phrases.shu.ac.uk/

Xrefer is a search engine that will answer questions by polling a large variety of reference sources.

- Xrefer
  www.xrefer.com

RESEARCH TOOLS

Daypop is a current events search engine that scans nearly 3000 news sites and web logs. Searches can be narrowed by time frames as small as three hours or as large as four weeks. It is a tool for locating new information and developments reported by news services and in web logs.

- Daypop
  www.daypop.com/

Electronic Journal Miner is a search engine designed to find magazines, newsletters, webzines or any serial published electronically. Journals can be found by title, keyword or Library of Congress Subject Heading. The engine was the result of the Electronic Journal Access Project developed by the Colorado Alliance of Research Libraries.

- Electronic Journal Miner
  ejournal.coalliance.org/

Find News Articles About People, Virtual Chase, September 2001 discusses various techniques for gathering news articles about people and finding background information using Internet and commercial online resources.

- Find News Articles About People
www.virtualchase.com/howto/news_search.html

Gateway to Associations Online is a database of over 6,000 associations provided by the American Society of Association Executives. Searches can be conducted by topic or name.

- Gateway to Associations Online
info.asaenet.org/gateway/OnlineAssocSlist.html

Get Cited is a literature search engine that contains indexing records for over three million books, journal articles and other research publications. It is also interactive, permitting scholars and researchers to guide in the development of the database.

- Get Cited
www.getcited.org/mbr/PUB/Find

Inequality.org is a socially conscious web site that provides information about under-publicized developments in the areas of economic change and progress.

- Inequality.org
www.inequality.org/

Infotrieve is a database service providing access to tables of contents from professional journals. One component is Article Finder, a free bibliographic database containing over 22 million citations and over 10 million abstracts from more than 35,000 of the most important scholarly journals in such areas as law, medicine and science. It also includes access to Medline, Publist and a Table of Contents alert service.

- Infotrieve
www4.infotrieve.com/home.asp

Insider's Guide to Criminal Justice Resources

Mag Portal is a search engine and news service that will ferret out individual magazine articles published on the web.

- Mag Portal
  www.magportal.com/

Pandia Radio Search is a powerful new search engine for locating TV and radio stations broadcasting over the web from all over the world.

- Pandia Radio Search
  www.pandia.com/radio/

RocketNews is a current news search engine that scans thousands of sources to find stories posted on the web in the previous five days. The news portal was created by RocketInfo, a search engine technology company.

- RocketNews
  www.rocketnews.com/
- RocketInfo
  www.rocketinfo.com/rocket/mainpage

SEARCH ENGINES

CompletePlanet is a unique search engine for locating documents in the "deep web," i.e., that part of the Internet not accessible to most search engines. The engine searches databases, not web pages per se, and produces a list of sites containing the search terms entered.

- CompletePlanet
  www.completeplanet.com/

Direct Search collects links to items not usually found using general search engines. It includes links to archives, libraries, bibliographies, government, news and legal resources.

- Direct Search
  gwis2.circ.gwu.edu/~gprice/direct.htm

Internet Archives: Preserving the History of Web Pages, LLRX, November 1, 2001 is an exploration of various sites dedicated to preserving the short-lived web pages and historical development of the Internet.

Most notable among the efforts is the Internet Archive Wayback Machine, containing over 100 terabytes and 10 billion web pages archived from 1996 to the present.

- Internet Archives: Preserving the History of Web Pages www.llrx.com/columns/webcritic12.htm
- Internet Archive Wayback Machine www.archive.org/index.html

Search Adobe PDF Online (Adobe Systems) is a unique search engine that will scan the web for PDF (portable document format) documents.

- Search Adobe PDF Online searchpdf.adobe.com/

SpeechBot is a new search engine from Compaq that locates audio content on the web. It currently indexes 9579 hours of content. Radio programs and a variety of broadcasts are searchable.

- SpeechBot speechbot.research.compaq.com/

Web Information Retrieval Tutorial is an extensive online slide show that describes and details the mystery behind the Google search engine.

- Web Information Retrieval Tutorial www.henzinger.com/monika/icde/icde-final_files/v3_document.htm
- Google www.google.com/

Web Search Engines FAQS, Searcher, October 2001 is a thorough examination of the workings behind popular search engines, dispelling misconceptions and pointing the way to the best use of these finding tools.

- Web Search Engines FAQS www.infotoday.com/searcher/oct01/price.htm

WebBrain.com is a graphical human edited search engine that enables web surfers to look for information in a unique way. It also offers a version of its interface for business or personal use.

- WebBrain.com
  www.webbrain.com/html/default_win.html

STATISTICS

Ameristat provides instant summaries of demographic characteristics of the U.S. population in such areas as race and ethnicity; income and poverty; and many others. It draws statistical data from many reliable sources, most notably the U.S. Census. Ameristat is sponsored by the Population Reference Bureau and the Social Science Data Analysis Network.

- Ameristat
  www.ameristat.org/

Census 2000 Data for the State of New York (US Census Bureau 2001). This is the results of the official Census New York State.

- Census 2000 Data for the State of New York www.census.gov/Press-Release/www/2001/tables/redist_ny.html

TERRORISM LAW

Criminal Enforcement Against Terrorists (Transactional Records Access Clearinghouse 2001). "The gap between the reported investigations and referrals for prosecution would appear to document a major challenge facing Law enforcement in its attempts to prevent terrorism and punish terrorists."

- Criminal Enforcement Against Terrorists
  trac.syr.edu/tracreports/terrorism/report011203.html

Upsetting Checks and Balances: Congressional Hostility Towards the Courts in Times of Crisis (ACLU 2001). "This report, planned long before September 11, focuses on the laws enacted five years ago rather than the USA-PATRIOT Act . . . . But enactment of the most recent anti-terrorism legislation provides new urgency for considering a theme common to all these laws: the role of the judiciary in curbing the excesses of executive authority in pursuit of politically popular goals . . . . This report is, in effect, a five-year report card on the country's ill-considered foray into court-stripping."

- Upsetting Checks and Balances: Congressional Hostility Towards the Courts in Times of Crisis www.aclu.org/congress/courtstripping.PDF

WEB TOOLS

Can't Afford a Web Designer? Do It Yourself, American Lawyer Media, October 3, 2001 is a helpful article for small firms or solo practitioners interested in creating a web site. It discusses simple and inexpensive options for self-publishing on the web.

- Can't Afford a Web Designer? Do it Yourself www.law.com/cgi-bin/gx.cgi/AppLogic+FTContentServer?pagename=law/View&c=Article&cid=ZZZGJFFWASC&live=true&cst=6&pc=0&pa=0&s=News&ExpIgnore=true&showsummary=0

Helping Bookmarks Fit Every Page, Technolawyer Community, August 6, 2001 is an article describing useful techniques and programs for managing a never-ending collection of Internet bookmarks.

- Helping Bookmarks Fit Every Page www.law.com/cgi-bin/gx.cgi/AppLogic+FTContentServer?pagename=law/View&c=Article&cid=ZZZZOOO3XPC&live=true&cst=6&pc=0&pa=0&s=News&ExpIgnore=true&showsummary=0

Home Page Reader, produced by IBM, is software that makes the Internet speak by translating the contents and elements of a web browser into human speech. For price information consult the product site.

- Home Page Reader www-3.ibm.com/able/hpr.html

Privacy.net provides a free analysis of information revealed through your Internet connection. It also promotes software and services to control the information disclosed as you surf the web.

- Privacy.net
  privacy.net/analyze

Shields Up! provides a free security analysis of computers connected to the web. It also promotes software and services to increase the security of files stored on your computer.

- Shields Up!
  grc.com/x/ne.dll?bhobkyd2

WeMedia Talking Web Browser can translate the web into human speech. The talking browser is designed to assist people with low vision or learning disabilities to use the Internet. Complete with large buttons and keystroke commands for easy navigation, the browser articulates selected text. The browser is available for free.

- WeMedia
  wemedia.com/

WRONGFUL CONVICTION

Commission on Proceedings Involving Guy Paul Morin (2v.) is a compilation of recent investigations focusing attention on the plight of the wrongfully convicted in the Canadian Justice System.

- Commission on Proceedings Involving Guy Paul Morin
  www.attorneygeneral.jus.gov.on.ca/html/MORIN/morin.htm

Convicted by Juries, Exonerated by Science: Case Studies in the Use of DNA Evidence to Establish Innocence After Trial is a collection of exculpatory case studies highlighting the value of DNA evidence to exonerate the innocent and the need for procedures and changes to assure accurate results.

- Convicted by Juries, Exonerated by Science:

Case Studies in the Use of DNA Evidence to Establish Innocence After Trial
www.ncjrs.org/pdffiles/dnaevid.pdf

False Memory Syndrome Foundation was founded by a group of families and professionals affiliated with the University of Pennsylvania and Johns Hopkins Medical Institution to document and study the problem of families that were being shattered when adult children suddenly claimed to have recovered repressed memories of childhood sexual abuse.

- False Memory Syndrome Foundation
www.fmsfonline.org/about.html

Innocence Project at Cardozo School of Law has retooled its web site. It contains case information, background materials on wrongful convictions, legislative developments, DNA news and links to resources. The Case Profiles database can be searched by name and other fields or the entire list can be viewed chronologically.

- Innocence Project at Cardozo School of Law
www.innocenceproject.org/

PART II

INTERNET RESOURCES COLLECTION

CONTENTS

APPELLATE PRACTICE 111
CASES, STATUTES AND REGULATIONS 111
CONTINUING LEGAL EDUCATION 120
CRIMINAL JUSTICE 121
DEATH PENALTY 123
DIRECTORIES AND LOCATORS 125
EXPERTS 129
FAMILY LAW 129
FORENSICS 130
IMMIGRATION 131
INTERNET INFORMATION 134
INTERNET SEARCHING 135
INTERPRETERS 137
INVESTIGATIVE TOOLS 138
JUVENILE JUSTICE 140
LEGAL RESEARCH 141
LEGAL SERVICES 145
LITIGATION 146
NEWS AND CURRENT AWARENESS 146
POST-CONVICTION 150
PRACTICE OF LAW 151
PROFESSIONAL RESPONSIBILITY 153
PUBLIC DEFENSE 154
REFERENCE MATERIALS 161
TERRORISM LAW 163

APPELLATE PRACTICE

■ Brief Banks

- Brief Bank Index (NACDL)
  www.nacdl.org/BriefBank.nsf/List
- Briefs in Recent and Landmark Cases (ACLU)
  www.aclu.org/court/court1.html
- National Amicus Curiae Briefs (ALSO)
  www.lawsource.com/also/usa.cgi?usb
- Rights International Brief Bank
  www.rightsinternational.org/ricenter/BriefBank/
- United States Supreme Court Briefs (Findlaw)
  supreme.findlaw.com/Supreme_Court/briefs/index.html

CASES, STATUTES AND REGULATIONS

■ Courts and Court Dockets

Researchers can find information about specific courts, a court system, docket information and a variety of databases containing appellate and lower court decisions.

- American Law Sources Online (U.S. Courts)
  www.lawsource.com
- Court Link
  www.courtlink.com/
- National Center for State Courts
  www.ncsc.dni.us/COURT/SITES/Courts.htm

Insider's Guide to Criminal Justice Resources

- National Judicial College
  www.judges.org/

- Your Nation's Courts Online
  www.courts.com

❑ **Federal and State Court Databases**

- LexisONE
  www.lexisone.com

- LoisLaw $
  www.loislaw.com

- VersusLaw $
  www.versuslaw.com/

❑ **United States Supreme Court**

- United States Supreme Court
  www.supremecourtus.gov/

- United States Supreme Court (LII)
  supct.law.cornell.edu/supct/index.html

- United States Supreme Court (Findlaw)
  www.findlaw.com/casecode/supreme.html

- United States Supreme Court News (NYSDA)
  www.nysda.org/Defense_News/defense_news.html#SupremeCourt

- Oyez Project at Northwestern University (Audio Files of Supreme Court Arguments)
  oyez.nwu.edu

❑ **Federal Courts**

Insider's Guide to Criminal Justice Resources

- United States Circuit Court of Appeals Search Engine (LII)
  www.law.cornell.edu:9999/USCA-ALL/results.html
- CourtWeb (District Court)
  www.nysd.uscourts.gov/courtweb/PubMain.htm
- PACER (Public Access to Electronic Court Records) $
  pacer.psc.uscourts.gov/
- Recent Civil Cases Filed in U.S. District Courts (Law.com)
  www.marketspan.com/states/LAWCOM/RecentCases.asp?Brand=LAWCOMLIT
- FedCrimLaw (Punch and Jurist) $
  www.fedcrimlaw.com/

❑ **New York Courts**

- New York State Court of Appeals (Official)
  www.courts.state.ny.us/ctapps/
- New York Court of Appeals (Legal Information Institute)
  www.law.cornell.edu/ny/ctap/overview.html
- New York Courts of Appeals Update (NYSDA—Robert Dean)
  www.nysda.org/Defense_News/defense_news.html#NYCCourtOfAppeals
- New York Court of Appeals and Legislative News
  www.nysda.org/Defense_News/defense_news.html#NYCCourtOfAppeals

Insider's Guide to Criminal Justice Resources

- Appellate Division, Fourth Department
  www.courts.state.ny.us/ad4/slips.html
- New York State Law Reporting Bureau
  www.courts.state.ny.us/reporter/
- E-Court (NY Criminal Dockets in 30 Counties)
  e.courts.state.ny.us/
- Decisions of Interest (NYLJ) $
  www6.law.com/ny/courts/courts.shtml
- New York Slip Opinion Service (Westlaw) $
  nyslip.westgroup.com/
- Select New York Criminal Law Cases (Buffalo Criminal Law Center)
  wings.buffalo.edu/law/bclc/web/nycaseixny.htm
- New York Court of Claims (Unpublished Opinions)
  nyscourtofclaims.state.ny.us/decision.htm
- New York State Supreme Court Library Queens
  www.courts.state.ny.us/queenslib/decisions.htm
- Monroe County Supreme Court
  www.frontiernet.net/~monsc/
- Judge Raymond E. Cornelius, Monroe County Supreme Court
  www.frontiernet.net/~derek/rec/rselect.htm
- Judge William C. Donnino, Bronx County Supreme Court
  ourworld.compuserve.com/homepages/w_c_d/

Insider's Guide to Criminal Justice Resources

- Judge Andrew V. Siracuse, Monroe County Supreme Court
  www.netacc.net/~amsir/Framework/Cases.html
- Library and Information Network (LION)
  www.courts.state.ny.us/LION/index.html
- Office of Court Administration (OCA)
  www.courts.state.ny.us/ucscoa.html
- Court Rules and Individual Judges' Rules for New York (State and Federal)
  www4.law.com/ny/rules/index.shtml
- New York Courts on the Web (NYLJ) $
  www.nycourts.com/
- NY Law Web Directory: Courts and Decisions (NYLJ)
  www4.law.com/ny/courts/
- New York Courts on the Web (OCA)
  www.courts.state.ny.us/ctpages.html
- New York Courts and Law Guide (NYLJ)
  www6.law.com/ny/guide/
- New York Courts (Findlaw)
  www.findlaw.com/11stategov/ny/courts.html

■ Statutes and Regulations

Read about new federal and state statutes. Learn about the activities of various agencies or find a statute concerning a defendant's predicate offense committed in another jurisdiction.

❑ **Federal Government**

- Thomas (Library of Congress)
  thomas.loc.gov
- House of Representatives
  www.house.gov/
- Senate
  www.senate.gov/

❏ **Constitution**

- United States Constitution (LII)
  www.law.cornell.edu/constitution/constitution.overview.html
- United States Constitution (Emory Law School)
  www.law.emory.edu/FEDERAL/usconst.html
- United States Constitution (Findlaw)
  www.findlaw.com/casecode/constitution/index.html

❏ **Federal Statutes**

- United States Code (GPO)
  www.access.gpo.gov/congress/cong013.html
- United States Code (House of Representatives)
  uscode.house.gov/usc.htm
- United States Code (LII)
  www4.law.cornell.edu/uscode/

- Public Laws (NARA)
  www.access.gpo.gov/nara/nara005.html

❑ **Federal Regulations**

- Code of Federal Regulations (NARA)
  www.access.gpo.gov/nara/cfr/index.html

- Federal Register (NARA)
  www.access.gpo.gov/su_docs/aces/aces140.html

❑ **Federal Resources**

- United States Government Manual (GPO)
  www.access.gpo.gov/nara/nara001.html

- Federal Information Center
  fic.info.gov/

- Government Information Locator Service (GPO)
  www.access.gpo.gov/su_docs/gils/index.html

- Fed World
  www.fedworld.gov/

- Federal Web Locator
  www.infoctr.edu/fwl/

❑ **State Laws**

- State Law (Findlaw)
  www.findlaw.com/casecode/state.html

Insider's Guide to Criminal Justice Resources

- Municipal Codes Online (Seattle Public Library)
  www.spl.org/selectedsites/municode.html
- Bill Tracking Resources, LLRX, August 15, 2000
  www.llrx.com/columns/roundup3.htm

❑ **Legislative News**

- Legislative Alerts (NACDL)
  www.criminaljustice.org/public.nsf/Free Form/Legislation?OpenDocument
- Government Relations (NLADA)
  www.nlada.org/Defender/Defender_Gov_Relations/Gov_DefenderAdvocacy_Home
- Legislative and Governmental Advocacy (ABA)
  www.abanet.org/poladv/home.html
- In Congress (ACLU)
  www.aclu.org/congress/
- GoverNet
  www.govaffairs.com/

❑ **New York Government**

- New York Assembly
  assembly.state.ny.us/
- New York Senate
  www.senate.state.ny.us/

- New York Bill Search (NY Assembly)
  assembly.state.ny.us/leg/
- New York Bill Search (NY Senate)
  leginfo.state.ny.us:82/INDEX1.html
- New York State Home Page
  www.state.ny.us/
- New York Government Information Locator Service
  www.nysl.nysed.gov/ils/
- New York Governor
  www.state.ny.us/governor/

❑ **New York Agencies**

- New York State Government Agencies
  www.state.ny.us/state_acc.html
- New York Attorney General
  www.oag.state.ny.us/
- New York Attorney General Opinions
  www.oag.state.ny.us/lawyers/opinions/opinion.html
- New York Division of Criminal Justice Services (DCJS)
  criminaljustice.state.ny.us/
- New York State Criminal Justice Agencies Directory (DCJS)
  criminaljustice.state.ny.us/crimnet/ojsa/agdir/htframe.htm

- New York Department of Correctional Services (DOCS)
  www.docs.state.ny.us/

- New York Division of Probation and Correction Alternatives
  dpca.state.ny.us/

- New York State Police
  www.troopers.state.ny.us/

- New York Unified Court System (OCA)
  www.courts.state.ny.us/

❑ **New York Laws**

- New York Constitution (NY Assembly)
  assembly.state.ny.us/leg/?co=0

- New York Consolidated Laws (NY Assembly)
  assembly.state.ny.us/leg/?cl=0

- New York Unconsolidated Laws (NY Assembly)
  assembly.state.ny.us/leg/?ul=0

- New York Chapter Laws (NY Assembly)
  assembly.state.ny.us/leg/?sl=0

CONTINUING LEGAL EDUCATION

Calendars of upcoming trainers, registration information and requirements for mandatory CLE credits are available online.

- ABA Center for CLE
  www.abanet.org/CLE/SITES.HTML

- Association for Continuing Legal Education
  www.aclea.org/
- MCLE State Requirements
  www.abanet.org/CLE/MCLEVIEW.HTML
- Washburn University School Seminars and Continuing Education
  www.washlaw.edu/postlaw/seminars.htm
- Westlaw Training Calendar
  www.westlaw.com/training/infocent.wl

❑ **New York**

- Mandatory Continuing Education (OCA)
  www.courts.state.ny.us/mcle.htm
- NYSDA Training Page
  www.nysda.org/Training/training.html
- NYSDA Training Calendar
  www.nysda.org/Training/Training_Calendars/training_calendars.html

CRIMINAL JUSTICE

- Criminal Justice Links
  www.criminology.fsu.edu/cj.html
- Hieros Gamos Guide to Criminal Law
  www.hg.org/crime.html
- Criminal Justice Mega-Links
  faculty.ncwc.edu/toconnor/
- Subject-based Internet Resources Criminal Justice and Law wally2.rit.edu/internet/subject/law.html

- Rand Corporation Abstracts
  www.rand.org/Abstracts/
- Transactional Records Access Clearinghouse (TRAC)
  trac.syr.edu/
- Vera Institute of Justice (VIJ)
  www.vera.org
- National Association of Sentencing Advocates' Sentencing Links
  www.sentencingproject.org/nasa/links.htm
- Criminal Justice Flow Chart
  www.ojp.usdoj.gov/bjs/justsys.htm

❑ **New York**

- Criminal Law Resources on the Internet (Buffalo Criminal Law Center) wings.buffalo.edu/law/bclc

■ **Criminal Justice Statistics**

- National Criminal Justice Reference Service
  www.ncjrs.org
- Bureau of Justice Statistics
  www.ojp.usdoj.gov/bjs/welcome.html
- Statistical Research
  www.virtualchase.com/resources/statistics.html#nacjs
- Sourcebook of Criminal Justice Statistics
  www.albany.edu/sourcebook/

❑ **New York**

- Criminal Justice Data for New York State
  criminaljustice.state.ny.us/crimnet/data.htm

DEATH PENALTY

Death Penalty News

- Capital Defense Weekly
  coramnobis.com/CDW/cdw.html
- Death Penalty Information Center's What's New
  www.deathpenaltyinfo.org/whatsnew.html
- NACDL Death Penalty Defense
  www.criminaljustice.org/public.nsf/freeform/DeathPenalty?OpenDocument

☐ **New York**

- NYSDA Capital Defense News
  www.nysda.org/Defense_Services/NY_Capital_Defense/ny_capital_defense.html
- New York Capital Defender Office
  www.nycdo.org/
- New Yorkers Against the Death Penalty
  www.nyadp.org/

Resources

Current developments, appellate litigation, manuals, motions and other resources can be found on several comprehensive death penalty web sites.

- Abolish Capital Punishment
  www.soci.niu.edu/~archives/ABOLISH/info.html

- Broken System: Error Rates in Capital Cases, 1973-1995 (Liebman)
  207.153.244.129/

- Capital Defender's Toolbox
  members.aol.com/karlkeys/index.html

- Capital Defense Network
  www.capdefnet.org

- Cornell University Law School's Death Penalty Project
  www.lawschool.cornell.edu/lawlibrary/death/default.htm

- Death Penalty Information Center
  www.deathpenaltyinfo.org/

■ International Law

Treaties and other international agreements that have a bearing on domestic cases, e.g., death penalty, can be located online.

- Hands Off Cain
  www.handsoffcain.org/

- International Law Emory
  www.law.emory.edu/FOCAL/intl.html

- ASIL Guide to Electronic Sources for International Law
  www.asil.org/resource/home.htm

- World List
  www.law.osaka-u.ac.jp/legal-info/worldlist/worldlst.htm

- Embassy Index
  www.embpage.org/

- International Web Site Index
  home.att.net/~slomansonb/intlweb.html
- International Human Rights Instruments
  www.unhchr.ch/html/intlinst.htm

DIRECTORIES AND LOCATORS

■ **Locating Tools**

- Webgator
  www.inil.com/users/dguss/wgator.htm
- Trackem People Search
  www.mdvl.net/~rcthomas/trackem.html

■ **Locating Lawyers**

- Martindale Hubbell's Lawyer Directory
  lawyers.martindale.com/marhub
- West's Legal Directory on Findlaw
  directory.findlaw.com/
- Hieros Gamos
  www.hg.org/attorney.html
- Best's Directory of Recommended Insurance Attorneys
  www.ambest.com/legal/atsearch.html

❑ **New York**

- New York State Office of Court Administration's Attorney Search
  www.courts.state.ny.us/webdb/wdbcgi.exe/apps/INTERNETDB.attyreghome.show

- New York State Chief Defenders List
  www.nysda.org/About_NYSDA/Chief_Defenders_A-M_/chief_defenders_a-m_.html

■ **Locating Judges**

Contact information for judges and government offices across the country can be found in these directories. Background information on judges is also available online.

- Judges of the United States Courts
  air.fjc.gov/history/judges_frm.html

- Directories of Courts and Judges (Duke University School of Law Library)
  www.law.duke.edu/lib/libser/publicat/researchGuides/courts/courtsframe.html

❏ **New York**

- Judges of the United States Court of Appeals for the Second Circuit
  www.tourolaw.edu/2ndcircuit/Info/Judges.htm

- Judge's Profiles (NYLJ)
  www4.law.com/ny/judges/index.shtml

- New York State Courts on the Web (OCA)
  www.courts.state.ny.us/ctpages.html

■ **Locating Inmates**

Learn about clients, co-defendants or witnesses who have been or are now in the state prison system.

- Federal Bureau of Prisons
  www.bop.gov/

Insider's Guide to Criminal Justice Resources

- Directory of Federal Detention Centers
  www.bop.gov/facilnot.html

❏ **New York**

- New York Inmate Lookup (DOCS)
  nysdocs.docs.state.ny.us:84/kinqw00
- New York Department of Correctional Services (DOCS)
  www.docs.state.ny.us/
- New York Correctional Services Directory (DOCS)
  www.docs.state.ny.us/faclist.html
- Map of New York Correctional Facilities (DOCS)
  www.docs.state.ny.us/jailmap.html
- New York State Criminal Justice Agencies Directory (DCJS)
  criminaljustice.state.ny.us/crimnet/ojsa/agdir/htframe.htm
- New York Division of Criminal Justice Services (DCJS)
  criminaljustice.state.ny.us/dcjs1.htm
- New York City Department of Corrections
  www.ci.nyc.ny.us/html/doc/home.html

■ **Locating People**

- AnyWho
  www.anywho.com
- AnyWho Reverse Lookup
  www.anywho.com/rl.html
- 555-1212
  www.555-1212.com

- Switchboard
  www.switchboard.com

- WhoWhere
  www.whowhere.lycos.com

- Ancestry.com
  www.ancestry.lycos.com

- Social Security Death Index
  www.ancestry.com/search/rectype/vital/ssdi/main.htm

- Find-A-Grave
  www.findagrave.com

■ Locating Prosecutors/Law Enforcement

- National District Attorneys Association
  www.ndaa.org

- Prosecutors' Web Sites
  www.co.eaton.mi.us/ecpa/proslist.htm

- National Association of Attorneys General
  www.naag.org

- Officer.com
  www.officer.com

- Law Enforcement Links
  www.leolinks.com/

- AELE Law Enforcement Legal Center
  www.aele.org/

EXPERTS

- National Directory of Expert Witnesses
  www.claims.com/
- Expert Pages
  expertpages.com
- Yearbook News
  www.yearbooknews.com/
- Midwest Directory of Expert Witnesses and Consultants
  www.texlaw.com/expert/center.htm
- Expert Witness Network
  www.witness.net
- Technical Advisory Service for Attorneys
  www.tasanet.com
- Expert Witnesses (Washlaw Web)
  www.washlaw.edu/expert.html

❑ **New York**

- New York City Assigned Counsel Expert Directory of Investigators and Experts (NYSDA)
  www.nysda.org/cgi-bin/baserun.cgi?_cfg=laser.cfg

FAMILY LAW

- ABA Section on Family Law
  www.abanet.org/family/home.html
- ABA Standards of Practice for Lawyers Representing a Child in Abuse and Neglect Cases
  www.abanet.org/child/childrep.html

- Family Law (LII)
  www.law.cornell.edu/topics/topic2.html#family law
- Uniform Matrimonial, Family, and Health Laws Locator
  www.law.cornell.edu/uniform/vol9.html
- Family Law and Social Policy Center at Syracuse University Law School
  www.law.syr.edu/academics/academics.asp?what=family_law_sp_center

❑ **New York**

- New York Divorce and Family Law
  www.brandeslaw.com/
- Family Court and You (NYSBA)
  www.nysba.org/public/famcourtandu.html
- Introductory Guide to the New York City Family Court
  www.courts.state.ny.us/famhome.htm
- Family Court Information Center Bronx and New York Counties
  www.courts.state.ny.us/kiosk/kiosk.htm
- Family Court Forms (OCA)
  www.courts.state.ny.us/famctforms/fcformtc.htm

FORENSICS

- Forensic Science Resources (Tennessee Association of Criminal Defense Lawyers)
  www.tncrimlaw.com/forensic/
- Zeno's Forensic Site
  forensic.to/forensic.html

Insider's Guide to Criminal Justice Resources

- Reference Manual on Scientific Evidence
  www.fjc.gov/EVIDENCE/science/sc_ev_sec.html
- Forensic Psychiatry Resource Page (University of Alabama)
  bama.ua.edu/~jhooper/
- American Board of Forensic Odontology
  www.abfo.org/
- American College of Forensic Examiners
  www.acfe.com/
- Johns Hopkins Autopsy Resource
  www.med.jhu.edu/pathology/iadb.html

IMMIGRATION

■ News

- Criminal Defense Immigration Project (NYSDA)
  www.nysda.org/NYSDA_Resources/Defense_Immigration_Project/defense_immigration_project.html
- Matthew Bender's Immigration Channel
  www.bender.com/bender/open/Webdriver?MIval=chan&channelID=immig
- Immigration Articles from The Champion (NACDL)
  www.criminaljustice.org/public.nsf/freeform/Immigration?OpenDocument

■ Federal Government

- United States Department of Labor Office of Administrative Law Judges Law Library
  www.oalj.dol.gov/libina.htm

- United States Department of Justice Executive Office for Immigration Review
  www.usdoj.gov/eoir/

- State Department's International Information Programs
  usinfo.state.gov/

- Bureau of Consular Affairs
  travel.state.gov/

■ **Immigration Law**

- Federal Immigration Law (LII)
  www.law.cornell.edu/topics/immigration.html

- Supreme Court Immigration Cases (LII)
  www4.law.cornell.edu/cgi-bin/fx?DB=SupctSyllabi&TOPDOC=0&P=immigration

- Federal Court Finder (Emory Law School)
  www.law.emory.edu/FEDCTS/

- United States Department of Labor Labor-Related Immigration Statute and Regulation Index
  www.oalj.dol.gov/public/ina/refrnc/istatin.htm

- Board of Immigration Appeals Precedent Decisions (BIA)
  www.usdoj.gov/eoir/efoia/bia/biaindx.htm

- Executive Office for Immigration Review OCAHO EFOIA Decisions
  www.usdoj.gov/eoir/efoia/ocaho/ocmnind.htm

- Immigration Law on the Web, LLRX (October 1, 1999)
  www.llrx.com/features/immigrat.htm

- Guide to Immigration and Legal Research on the Internet
  www.ailapubs.org/ailguidtoima.html

Immigration Organizations

- American Immigration Lawyers Association
  www.aila.org/
- Amnesty International
  www.amnesty.org/
- ACLU Immigrant's Rights
  www.aclu.org/issues/immigrant/hmir.html
- Central American Refugee Center
  www.icomm.ca/carecen/
- Citizens and Immigrants for Equal Justice
  www.angelfire.com/tx/equalrights/index.html
- National Immigration Forum
  www.immigrationforum.org/
- National Immigration Law Center
  www.nilc.org/
- National Lawyers Guild/National Immigration Project
  www.nlg.org/nip/
- National Network for Immigrant and Refugee Rights
  www.nnirr.org/
- Lawyers Committee for Human Rights
  www.lchr.org/home.htm

Immigration Reference Sources

Insider's Guide to Criminal Justice Resources

- Country Reports on Human Rights Practices (DOS)
  www.state.gov/www/global/human_rights/hrp_reports_mainhp.html

- CIA World Factbook
  www.odci.gov/cia/publications/factbook/

- RefWorld
  www.unhcr.ch/research/rsd.htm

- State Department's Bureau of Democracy, Human Rights, and Labor
  www.state.gov/www/global/human_rights/

- International Journal of Refugee Law
  www3.oup.co.uk/reflaw/

INTERNET INFORMATION

■ Background and Terminology

- Using and Understanding the Internet
  www.pbs.org/uti/

- Finding Information on the Internet
  www.lib.berkeley.edu/TeachingLib/Guides/Internet

- Third Age Internet Glossary
  www.thirdage.com/features/tech/glossary/index.html

- Bibliography of Internet Books (ABA)
  www.abanet.org/lpm/magazine/booklist.html

■ Internet Service Providers

- Internet Access
  webisplist.internetlist.com/

Insider's Guide to Criminal Justice Resources

- The List
  thelist.internet.com/

■ **Web Tools**

- Netscape
  www.netscape.com

- Microsoft's Internet Explorer
  www.microsoft.com/ie

- Adobe Acrobat Reader
  www.adobe.com

- WeMedia (Talking Web Browser)
  www.wemedia.com

- IBM Home Page Reader $
  www-3.ibm.com/able/hpr.html

■ **Email**

- E-Mail Communication for Client Matters -- A Multinational Survey (LegalEthics.com 2000)
  www.legalethics.com/articles.law?auth=intnl.txt

- Don't Throw Away the Attorney-Client Privilege, New Jersey Law Journal, May 2, 2001
  www.law.com/cgi-bin/gx.cgi/AppLogic+FTContentServer?pagename=law/View&c=Article&cid=ZZZ24EI07MC&live=true&cst=6&pc=0&pa=0&s=News&ExpIgnore=true&showsummary=0

INTERNET SEARCHING

■ **Search Engines**

- LawCrawler
  www.lawcrawler.com

- LawRunner
  www.lawrunner.com

- Google
  www.google.com

- Alta Vista
  www.altavista.com

- Hotbot
  www.hotbot.com

■ Directories

- Findlaw
  www.findlaw.com

- Jeff Flax's Web Page: Focusing on Legal Resources on the Internet
  www.jflax.com

- Yahoo
  www.yahoo.com

■ Meta-Indexes

- American Law Sources Online (ALSO)
  www.lawsource.com

- Dogpile
  www.dogpile.com

- Metafind
  www.metafind.com/

- **Natural Language Tool**
  - Ask Jeeves
    www.askjeeves.com
- **New Search Tools**
  - Search Engine Watch
    www.searchenginewatch.com/
  - Search Engine Showdown
    www.notess.com/search/
  - CNET
    www.cnet.com
  - ZD (Ziff Davis) Net
    www.zdnet.com
  - PC Magazine
    www.pcmagazine.com

INTERPRETERS

- **Translation Services Online**
  - AltaVista Babel Fish
    babelfish.altavista.com/
  - Babylon Translation
    babylon.com
  - Free Translation
    www.freetranslation.com
- **Locating Interpreters**

- Language Line Services
  www.languageline.com

- Court Interpretation Standards (National Center for State Courts)
  www.ncsc.dni.us/research/interp/

❏ **New York**

- Court Interpreter Manual (U.S. District Court Northern District of New York)
  www.nynd.uscourts.gov/forms/courtint.pdf

INVESTIGATIVE TOOLS

Beyond legal research, the web is an excellent tool for developing factual information to be used in court. Reverse Phone Directories, maps and public records are only a few examples of the resources available.

■ **Associations**

- National Defender Investigation Association
  ndia-inv.org/

■ **Crime Scenes**

- Crime Scene Investigations
  www.feinc.net/cs-inv.htm

- Crime Scene Investigation
  www.crime-scene-investigator.net/index.html

■ **Freedom of Information**

- Freedom of Information Act Resources (Society of Professional Journalists)
  www.spj.org/foia.asp

Insider's Guide to Criminal Justice Resources

- Freedom of Information Resources (Professor Fought, Syracuse University)
  web.syr.edu/~bcfought/
- Freedom of Information Act (DOJ)
  www.usdoj.gov/foia

❑ **New York**

- New York Committee on Open Government Advisory Opinions
  dos.state.ny.us/coog/findex.html

■ **Maps and Directions**

- Mapquest
  www.mapquest.com/
- Yahoo Maps and Driving Directions
  maps.yahoo.com/py/maps.py
- Lycos Roadmaps
  www.lycos.com/roadmap.html
- Maps On Us
  www.mapsonus.com
- Internet Travel Network
  www.itn.com
- Amtrak
  www.amtrak.com
- MIT Geographic Name Server
  sipb-server-1.mit.edu/geo?location
- Geographic Names Information System
  mapping.usgs.gov/www/gnis/gnisform.html

Insider's Guide to Criminal Justice Resources

- **Public Records**
  - DocuSearch
    www.docusearch.com/free.html
  - BRB Publications
    www.brbpub.com
  - Public Records
    www.pac-info.com/
  - Vital Records Information
    www.vitalrec.com
  - VitalChek
    www.vitalchek.com/
  - Accurint $
    www.accurint.com
  - 1-800-US Search $
    www.1800ussearch.com
  - KnowX.com $
    www.knowx.com

- **Weather**
  - National Climatic Data Center
    www.ncdc.noaa.gov/
  - Docu-Weather $
    www.weather-claims.com

JUVENILE JUSTICE

  - ABA Juvenile Justice Center
    www.abanet.org/crimjust/juvjus/home.html

Insider's Guide to Criminal Justice Resources

- Juvenile Justice (LII)
  www.law.cornell.edu/topics/juvenile.html
- United States Office of Juvenile Justice and Delinquency Prevention
  ojjdp.ncjrs.org
- National Center for Juvenile Justice
  www.ncjj.org/
- Juvenile Information Network
  www.juvenilenet.org/
- National Council of Juvenile and Family Court Judges
  www.ncjfcj.unr.edu/

LEGAL RESEARCH

■ Law Libraries

Most law libraries have online catalogs that can be accessed through the web. In addition to saving time in locating materials, these catalogs often include links to periodical databases and other indexes.

- Law Library Catalogs (Washlaw Web)
  www.washlaw.edu/lawcat/lawcat.html
- Library of Congress
  www.loc.gov/z3950/
- National Equal Justice Library
  library.wcl.american.edu/nejl/

❑ **New York**

- John Jay College Library of Criminal Justice
  www.lib.jjay.cuny.edu/index.html

- Legal Aid Society of New York
  www.legal-aid.org/lib.htm
- New York State Library
  www.nysl.nysed.gov/index.html

■ Law Publishers and Vendors

- Publist
  www.publist.com
- American Lawyer Media
  www.lawcatalog.com/
- BNA
  www.bna.com
- ForeCite (Criminal Jury Instructions)
  www.forecite.com
- James Publishing
  www.jamespublishing.com/
- Matthew Bender
  www.bender.com
- West Group
  www.westgroup.com
- LawBook Exchange
  www.lawbookexc.com

❏ **New York**

- Blumberg
  www.blumberg.com/index.html

- Gould Publishing
  www.gouldlaw.com
- Hein Publishing
  www.wshein.com/
- New York Legal Publishing
  www.nylp.com/
- New York State Bar Association
  www.nysba.org/public/public.html

■ **Law Reviews**

- Full Text Search of Journals on Internet (Findlaw)
  stu.findlaw.com/journals/
- Contents Pages from Law Reviews and Other Scholarly Journals (University of Texas Law School)
  tarlton.law.utexas.edu/tallons/content_search.html
- Anderson Publishing's 1999 On-Line Directory of Law Reviews and Scholarly Legal Periodicals
  www.andersonpublishing.com/lawschool/directory/

❏ **New York**

- New York State Bar Journal
  www.nysba.org/media/barjournal/journalindex.html
- Buffalo Criminal Law Review (Buffalo Criminal Law Center) wings.buffalo.edu/law/bclc/bclr.htm
- Buffalo Law Review
  wings.buffalo.edu/academic/department/law/blr/
- Journal of Criminal Justice and Popular Culture
  www.albany.edu/scj/jcjpc/index.html

Insider's Guide to Criminal Justice Resources

- Touro Law Review
  www.tourolaw.edu/Publications/Lawreview/

■ **Law Schools**

- ABA Approved
  www.abanet.org/legaled/approvedlawschools/approved.html

- American Association of Law Schools
  www.aals.org/

- Directory of Legal Academia
  www.law.cornell.edu/dla/

- Legal Education and Admission to the Bar
  www.abanet.org/Legaled/Home.Html

- Law Schools (Internet Legal Resource Guide)
  www.ilrg.com/schools.html

- United States Law Schools on the Web (University of Kansas School of Law)
  www.law.ukans.edu/library/usschools.html

■ **Lexis**

- Lexis MVP Program
  web.lexis.com/xchange/marketplace/MVPforSmallLawFirms.asp

- National Legal Aid and Defender Association Discount Program
  www.nlada.org/Member_Svcs/MemberSvcs_Benefits#discounts

- Legal Services Corporation Discount Program
  www.equaljustice.org/techno/lexis.htm
- Lexis Pay as You Go
  www.lexisone.com/legalresearch/payasyougo/index.html

❑ **New York**

- Association of the Bar of the City of New York Lexis Discount Program
  www.abcny.org/memserv2.html#reference
- New York State Bar Association Lexis Discount Program
  www.nysba.org/member/LexisNexis.html

■ **Westlaw**

- Westlaw Subscription Options
  www.westlaw.com/SubOptions/
- Westlaw Pro
  www.westlaw.com/SubOptions/lawfirm.wl

❑ **New York**

- Westlaw Pro New York
  www.westlaw.com/SubOptions/WestlawPro/States/nywlpro.wl

LEGAL SERVICES

- Handsnet
  www.handsnet.org
- Legal Associations and Organizations (Findlaw)
  www.findlaw.com/06associations/index.html

- Legal Service Organizations (Pine Tree Legal Assistance)
  www.ptla.org/links.htm

- National Center on Poverty Law
  www.povertylaw.org

LITIGATION

- Case Central
  www.casecentral.com/home.htm

- Lights, Camera, Verdict, New York Law Journal, September 13, 1999
  www.nylj.com/tech/091399t2.html

NEWS AND CURRENT AWARENESS

■ Legal News

National and local developments in the law, as well as the latest news about legislation and court decisions can be found in online legal newspapers or at criminal defense organization web sites. Many of these sites contain archives of old news stories.

- American Bar Association Journal
  www.abanet.org/journal/home.html

- Champion (NACDL)
  www.criminaljustice.org/public.nsf/FreeForm/ChampionMag?OpenDocument

- Court TV
  www.courttv.com

- CrimeLynx Today
  www.crimelynx.com/

- Current News Releases (NACDL)
  www.criminaljustice.org/PUBLIC/news.htm
- Findlaw Legal News
  news.findlaw.com/
- Law.com
  www.law.com
- National Association of Criminal Defense Lawyers News
  www.nacdl.org/public.nsf/freeform/news&issues?OpenDocument
- National Law Journal
  www.nlj.com
- Wire: Prison Related News
  www.sfsu.edu/~tamamail/wire.html

❑ **New York**

- New York Defense News (NYSDA)
  www.nysda.org/Defense_News/defense_news.html
- New York Law Journal
  www.nylj.com
- New York State Assembly
  assembly.state.ny.us/Press/
- New York State Governor
  www.state.ny.us/governor/
- New York State Senate
  www.senate.state.ny.us/press.html
- New York Court System (OCA)
  www.courts.state.ny.us/newsevent2.html

Insider's Guide to Criminal Justice Resources

■ **National, State and Local News**

Find your local newspaper online. Most television, radio and print news services have web sites with full text copies of their latest stories.

- NewsDirectory.com
  www.newsdirectory.com

- Yahoo! Broadcast
  www.broadcast.com

- Television News Archive (Vanderbilt University)
  tvnews.vanderbilt.edu/

- 1st Headline News
  www.1stheadlines.com/

- Free News Index
  www.newsindex.com/freenews.html

- AP Wire
  wire.ap.org/

- Moreover
  w.moreover.com/

- Electric Library
  wwws.elibrary.com/id/238/100/search.cgi?id=

- Editorial Opinion Pages
  www.opinion-pages.org/united_states.htm

❑ **New York**

- New York Wired
  www.newyorkwired.com/

- Empire Page
  www.empirepage.com/
- Gotham Gazette (NYC)
  www.gothamgazette.com/
- New York News Papers Online (NewsDirectory.com)
  www.newsdirectory.com/news/press/na/us/ny/

■ **E-Bulletins**

Receive summaries and news concerning recent Supreme Court, federal and state court decisions by email.

- United States Supreme Court E-Bulletin (LII)
  www.law.cornell.edu/focus/bulletins.html
- Supreme Court News and Decisions (Willamette University College of Law)
  www.willamette.edu/wucl/wlo/us-supreme/
- Legal Newswire
  www.lawnewsnetwork.com/newswire/
- Findlaw Newsletters
  newsletters.findlaw.com/
- Moreover.com Newsletters
  www.moreover.com

❑ **New York**

- New York Court of Appeals E-Bulletin (LII)
  www.law.cornell.edu/bulletin/index.htm

◼ Listservs

Listservs are forums where practitioners and academics share ideas, pose questions and discuss issues and resources related to particular topics, such as the Death Penalty, forensics and psychiatry.

- ABA Network
  www.abanet.org/discussions/home.html

- Equal Justice Network
  www.equaljustice.org/connections/listoflists.htm#access

- Findlaw's Legal Minds
  www.legalminds.org/

- Law Lists (University of Chicago Law School)
  www.lib.uchicago.edu/~llou/lawlists/info.html

- Stetson University College of Law
  www.law.stetson.edu/law/

- Tennessee Criminal Law Defense Resources Criminal and Law Links
  www.tncrimlaw.com/crimlist.html

POST-CONVICTION

◼ Habeas Corpus

- Federal Habeas Corpus Review (Findlaw)
  findlaw.com/habeas/index.html

- New Habeas Act: AEDPA (Findlaw)
  findlaw.com/habeas/checklist.html

Insider's Guide to Criminal Justice Resources

- Capital Defense Network's Habeas Assistance and Training
  www.capdefnet.org/hat/contents/hat_webcontents.htm

PRACTICE OF LAW

■ Employment

- EmployerNet (Lexis-Nexis)
  www.employernet.com/index.cfm
- Equal Justice Network
  www.equaljustice.org/jobs/index.html
- Job Links for Lawyers
  home.sprynet.com/~ear2ground/
- Jurist
  jurist.law.pitt.edu/position.htm
- Legal Employment Search Site
  www.legalemploy.com
- NLADA Job Opportunities
  www.nlada.org/jobop.htm

❑ **New York**

- NYSDA Jobs
  www.nysda.org/Contact_Us/Jobs/jobs.html

■ Law Office Management

- Management Information Exchange
  www.m-i-e.org/
- Mind Manager
  www.mindmanager.com

- The Brain
  www.thebrain.com

- New Way to Manage Law Firm Knowledge, New York Law Journal, January 24, 2000
  www.nylj.com/tech/012400t1.html

■ Law Office Supplies

- Biz Buyer
  www.bizbuyer.com/default.asp?sourceID=3866

- Office Depot
  www.officedepot.com

- Office Max
  www.officemax.com/FreeDelivery/catalog.html

- Staples
  www.staples.com

■ Law Office Technology

- Dennis Kennedy's Legal Technology Primer
  www.denniskennedy.com/ltprimer.htm

- LawyerWare
  www.lawyerware.com/

- Micro Law
  www.microlaw.com/

- Law Technology News
  www.lawtechnews.com/

- Technology Surveys (ABA)
  www.abanet.org/tech/ltrc/surveys/home.html

New York

- GungaWeb: Web-Based Analysis of New York State Criminal Law
  www.gungaweb.com

- Crime Time (Tompkins County DA)
  www.tompkins-co.org/distatto/CrimeTime.html

PowerPoint

- Presenters Online
  www.presentersonline.com

- Element K Journals
  www.elementkjournals.com/

- Presenters University
  www.presentersuniversity.com/default.cfm

- PowerPoint Master Class
  www.zdnet.com/anchordesk/story/story_4542.html

Strategic Planning

- Strategic Planning for Information Technology (Center for Computer-Assisted Legal Instruction)
  www.cali.org/jlsc/molina.html

- Strategic Planning Report: Indigent Defense Committee Wisconsin Bar Association
  www.wisbar.org/bar/provision/reports/indigent.html

PROFESSIONAL RESPONSIBILITY

Conflicts of interest, confidentiality and other ethical questions can be answered by examining bar association ethics codes and opinions online.

- Legal Ethics Resource Guide (Cornell University School of Law)
  www.lawschool.cornell.edu/lawlibrary/finding_the_law/guides_by_topic/ethics.htm
- FindLaw Ethics Guide
  www.findlaw.com/01topics/14ethics/index.html
- LegalEthics.com
  www.legalethics.com/ethicsites.htm

❑ **New York**

- New York State Bar Association Ethics Opinions
  www.nysba.org/opinions/opinions.html
- Association of the Bar of the City of New York Ethics Opinions
  www.abcny.org/eth1999.htm
- New York County Lawyers Association Ethics Opinions
  www.nycla.org/library/ethics.htm
- Nassau County Bar Association Ethics Opinions
  www.nassaubar.org/ethic_opinions.cfm
- Suffolk County Bar Association Ethics Opinions
  www.scba.org/ethics_opinions.html

PUBLIC DEFENSE

Criminal defense and related organizations publish newsletters and articles, reports on current issues, motions and briefs, training calendars and standards of practice. They post links to web sites on criminal law research, such as forensics or the death penalty. Information about joining assigned counsel panels, training and eligibility requirements is also available.

Insider's Guide to Criminal Justice Resources

- **National**
  - National Association of Criminal Defense Lawyers (NACDL)
    www.nacdl.org
  - National Legal Aid and Defender Association (NLADA)
    www.nlada.org
  - American Civil Liberties Union (ACLU)
    www.aclu.org/
  - American Civil Liberties Affiliate Directory
    www.aclu.org/community/community.html
  - Amnesty International (AI)
    www.amnestyusa.org/
  - Equal Justice Network
    www.equaljustice.org
  - Human Rights Watch (HRW)
    www.hrw.org/

- **Federal**
  - Association of Federal Defense Attorneys
    www.afda.org/new/
  - Web Sites for Federal Defenders
    www.geocities.com/fpdweb/

- **State**
  - Georgia Indigent Defense Council
    www.gidc.com/

Insider's Guide to Criminal Justice Resources

- Kentucky Department of Public Advocacy
  dpa.state.ky.us/
- Lake County Public Defender (IL)
  www.co.lake.il.us/PUBDEF/INDEX.HTM
- Louisiana Indigent Defender Board
  www.lidb.com/
- Michigan State Appellate Defender Office
  www.sado.org/
- Tennessee Criminal Law Defense Resources
  www.tncrimlaw.com/

❑ **New York**

- New York State Defenders Association (NYSDA)
  www.nysda.org
- New York State Association of Criminal Defense Lawyers
  www.nysacdl.org/
- Albany County Public Defenders Office
  www.albanycounty.com/departments/publicdefender/
- Association of Assigned Counsel (NYC)
  www.internet-esq.com/ny18-b.htm
- Brooklyn Defender Services
  www.bds.org
- Capital Defender Office
  www.nycdo.org/
- Cayuga County Assigned Counsel Program
  co.cayuga.ny.us/counsel/index.html

Insider's Guide to Criminal Justice Resources

- Cortland County Public Defender
  www2.cortland-co.org/pubdef/public%20defender.htm
- Erie County Bar Association Aid to Indigent Prisoners Society
  assigned.org/
- Jefferson County Public Defender
  www.sunyjefferson.edu/JC/Services/Departments/pubdef.html
- Legal Aid Society of New York
  www.legal-aid.org
- Monroe County Assigned Counsel Program
  www.mcacp.org
- Neighborhood Defender Service
  www.ndsny.org/
- Office of the Appellate Defender (NYC)
  www.appellatedefender.org/
- Orleans County Public Defender
  www.orleansny.com/pubdef.htm
- Steuben County Public Defender
  www.steubencony.org/pubdef.html
- Tompkins County Assigned Counsel Program
  people.clarityconnect.com/webpages2/ir/be0raab1.htm

■ **Assigned Counsel Rates**
  ❑ **New York**

- Assigned Counsel Rates (NYSDA)
  www.nysda.org/Hot_Topics/Assigned_Counsel_Rates/assigned_counsel_rates.html

- Resolving the Assigned Counsel Fee Crisis: An Opportunity to Provide County Fiscal Relief and Quality Public Defense Services (NYSDA 2001)
  www.nysda.org/ResolvingtheAssignedCounselFeeCrisis_01.pdf

- Determining Eligibility for Appointed Counsel in New York State (NYSDA)
  www.nysda.org/Publications/NYSDA_Reports_Studies/TOC_NYSDAEligibilityReport.htm

■ **Criminal Defense Practice**

❏ **New York**

- Criminal Defendant Handbook (OCA)
  www.courts.state.ny.us/Handcrimdef.html

- What You Should Know If You Accused of a Crime (Joyce B. David)
  www.getty.net/texts/law-1.txt

- Criminal Court of the City of New York
  www.courts.state.ny.us/crim0498.htm

- How to Read the New York State Rap Sheet
  criminaljustice.state.ny.us/crimnet/cust/rapsheet.pdf

- New York State Criminal Justice Agencies
  criminaljustice.state.ny.us/crimnet/ojsa/agdir/agencydr.pdf

■ **Indigent Defense Systems**

Insider's Guide to Criminal Justice Resources

- Spangenberg Group
  www.spangenberggroup.com/
- Spangenberg Group Publications
  www.spangenberggroup.com/pub.html
- Spangenberg Group Newsletters
  www.spangenberggroup.com/tsg_report.html
- Comparative Analysis of Indigent Defense Expenditures and Caseloads in States with Mixed State and County Funding (Spangenberg Group 1998)
  www.gidc.com/spangen.htm
- Indigent Defense Systems in the United States, 58 Law and Contemporary Problems 1 (1995) (Spangenberg Group)
  www.pili.org/library/access/law_and_contemporary_problems.htm

❑ **New York**

- Defense Standards (NYSDA)
  www.nysda.org/Defense_Services/defense_services.html
- New York Capital Defense (NYSDA)
  www.nysda.org/Defense_Services/NY_Capital_Defense/ny_capital_defense.html
- Public Defense Data (NYSDA)
  www.nysda.org/NYSDA_Resources/Public_Defense_Data/public_defense_data.html
- Public Defense Providers (NYSDA)
  www.nysda.org/Defense_Services/defense_services.html

- Structure of the Public Defense Systems in New York State (NYSDA)
  www.nysda.org/Defense_Services/NY_Indigent_Defense_Structure/ny_indigent_defense_structure.html
- Technical Studies, Model Forms and Other Reports (NYSDA)
  www.nysda.org/NYSDA_Resources/Public_Defense_Data/public_defense_data.html

Standards

- ABA Division of Legal Services
  www.ambar.org/legalservices/
- Compendium of Standards for Indigent Defense Systems (BJA)
  www.ojp.usdoj.gov/indigentdefense/compendium/
- Indigent Defense Standards and Guidelines Index (ABA)
  www.ambar.org/legalservices/indefstd.txt
- Defense Standards Links (NYSDA)
  www.nysda.org/Defense_Services/defense_services.html
- Standards (NLADA)
  www.nlada.org/Defender/Defender_Standards/Defender_Standards_Home
- Standards and Guidelines (NACDL)
  www.criminaljustice.org/indigent/guides.htm
- Standards for Death Penalty Cases And Civil Legal Service (ABA)
  www.abanet.org/legalservices/divhomedownload.html

Insider's Guide to Criminal Justice Resources

REFERENCE MATERIALS

- **Reference Tools**
    - Legal and Law Reference Site
      www.mnsfld.edu/depts/lib/mu-ref.html
    - Reference Desk
      www.refdesk.com
    - Research-It!
      www.itools.com/research-it/
    - Virtual Library Reference Desk
      www.washlaw.edu/reflaw/reflaw.html
    - Washlaw Web
      www.washlaw.edu/reflaw/reflaw.html

- **Encyclopedias**
    - Columbia Encyclopedia
      www.bartleby.com/65/
    - Encyclopedia Britannica $
      www.britannica.com
    - Legal Research Encyclopedia (Cornell University School of Law)
      www.lawschool.cornell.edu/lawlibrary/encyclopedia/
    - ❏ **New York**
    - New York Courts and Law Guide
      www6.law.com/ny/guide/

- **Dictionaries**

- Cambridge Dictionaries Online
  dictionary.cambridge.org/

- Dictionary.com
  www.dictionary.com

- Law Dictionary
  dictionary.law.com/

- Merriam-Webster
  www.m-w.com

- Nolo's Law Dictionary
  www.nolo.com/dictionary/wordindex.cfm

- Quotations
  quotations.miningco.com/arts/quotations/

- Thesaurus
  www.thesaurus.com

- YourDictionary.com
  www.yourdictionary.com

■ **Language and Style Manuals**

- Strunk and White's Elements of Style
  www.bartleby.com/141/index.html

■ **Medical Information**

- American Medical Association (AMA)
  www.ama-assn.org

- Free Medical Journals
  www.freemedicaljournals.com/

- Lab Tests Online
  www.labtestsonline.org/
- Medical Specialty Organization Index
  www.msmnet.com/resources/specialty.htm
- MedicineNet
  www.medicinenet.com
- Medline
  www.mdicinenet.com
- Merck Manual
  www.merck.com/pubs/mmanual/sections.htm
- Pharma-Lexicon: A Dictionary of Pharmaceutical Medicine
  www.pharma-lexicon.com/

TERRORISM LAW

This is a compilation of laws and executive and administrative orders enacted since September 11th, as well as other relevant existing laws. News, reports, guides and research links to current sources of information are also included.

■ National Legislation and Orders

- U.S.A. Patriot Act of 2001, Public Law No. 107-56 (H.R.3162)
  thomas.loc.gov/cgi-bin/bdquery/z?d107:h.r.03162:

- Monitoring Attorney-Client Communications - Federal Bureau of Prisons: National Security; Prevention of Acts of Violence and Terrorism; Final Rule (October 31, 2001)
  frwebgate.access.gpo.gov/cgi-bin/getdoc.cgi?dbname=2001_register&docid=01-27472-filed.pdf

- Military Tribunals-Military Order: Detention, Treatment, and Trial of Certain Non-Citizens in the War Against Terrorism, Presidential Order (November 13, 2001)
  www.whitehouse.gov/news/releases/2001/11/20011113-27.html

- Public Law No: 107-40. A Joint Resolution to Authorize the Use of United States Armed Forces Against Those Responsible for the Recent Attacks Launched Against the United States
  thomas.loc.gov/cgi-bin/bdquery/z?d107:SJ00023:|TOM:/bss/d107query.htm

- Title 10 USC Armed Forces (U.S. House of Representatives)
  uscode.house.gov/title_10.htm

- Title 10 USC Chapter 47: Uniform Code of Military Justice (U.S. House of Representatives)
  uscode.house.gov/DOWNLOAD/10C47.DOC

- Ex Parte Quirin , 317 U.S. 1 (1942). (Denial of habeas corpus action challenging detention of petitioners by military commission, appointed by the Order of the President of July 2, 1942, for violating the Articles of War)
  laws.findlaw.com/us/317/1.html

■ **National Legislative and Administrative Resources**

- Federal Legislation Related to the Attack of September 11, 2001 (Thomas)
  thomas.loc.gov/home/terrorleg.htm

- DOJ Response to Terrorist Attacks
  www.usdoj.gov/ag/terrorismaftermath.html

- DOJ Oversight: Preserving Our Freedoms While Defending Against Terrorism (Senate Committee on the Judiciary Hearing November 28, 2001)
  judiciary.senate.gov/hr112801f.htm

- Terrorism Measures and Related NLADA Materials (NLADA)
  www.nlada.org/Defender/Shared/Terrorism

■ **New York Legislation and Orders**

- Anti-Terrorism Act of 2001
  www.nysda.org/Defense_News/NYAntiTerrorismAct2001.pdf

- World Trade Center Emergency Executive Orders
  www.state.ny.us/sept11/wtc_exeorders.html

■ **New York Legislative and Administrative Resources**

- How to Trace New York State Regulations and Executive Orders (Albany Law School)
  www.als.edu/lib/als_nyre.html
- New York State Disaster and Terrorism Legislation for 2001 (LLRX)
  www.llrx.com/features/nydisaster.htm

■ **Reports**

- Criminal Enforcement Against Terrorists (Transactional Records Access Clearinghouse 2001)
  trac.syr.edu/tracreports/terrorism/report011203.html
- Upsetting Checks and Balances: Congressional Hostility Towards the Courts in Times of Crisis (ACLU 2001)
  www.aclu.org/congress/courtstripping.PDF

■ **Resources**

- 9-11-2001 News and Legal Resources, Information and Related Services (LLRX)
  www.llrx.com/newstand/wtc.htm
- ABA Disaster Legal Services
  www.abanet.org/legalservices/disaster.html
- ABA Task Force on Terrorism and the Law
  www.abanet.org/journal/dec01/awash.html
- Bibliography on Terrorism, Bioterrorism, the Middle East, and 9-11 Related Issues (LLRX)
  www.llrx.com/features/terrorbiblio.htm
- Bureau of Consular Affairs (DOS)
  www.travel.state.gov/

- Civil Liberties (Yahoo)
  dailynews.yahoo.com/fc/US/Civil_Liberties/
- Documents in Civil and Criminal Cases (Findlaw)
  news.findlaw.com/legalnews/us/terrorism/cases/index.html
- Fighting Terrorism/Protecting Liberty (NACDL)
  www.nacdl.org/public.nsf/freeform/terrorism1?opendocument
- Immigration Reference Materials Related to September 11 Terrorist Attack (American Immigration Law Foundation)
  www.ailf.org/911/
- Multi-Lingual "Know Your Rights!" Pamphlet to Educate Public (ACLU)
  www.aclu.org/news/2001/n111401a.html
- National Security (ACLU)
  www.aclu.org/issues/security/hmns.html
- New York City Legal Aid Society WTC Related Updates and Guides
  www.legal-aid.org/
- New York State Unified Court System
  www.courts.state.ny.us/
- Newslib Research Queries
  www.ibiblio.org/journalism/NWSworldtradecenter.html
- Post-September 11 Environment: Access to Government Information (OMB Watch)
  www.ombwatch.org/info/2001/access.html

Insider's Guide to Criminal Justice Resources

- Question of Balance (Law.com)
  www.law.com/cgi-bin/gx.cgi/AppLogic+FTContentServer?pagename=law/View&c=Article&cid=ZZZGKFMUTRC&live=true&cst=1&pc=0&pa=0&s=News&ExpIgnore=true&showsummary=0

- Safe and Free Clearinghouse (ACLU)
  www.aclu.org/safeandfree/index.html

- September 11 Archive (LOC)
  september11.archive.org/

- September 11 Tragedy (Empire Page)
  www.empirepage.com/911/index.html

- Special Coverage: War on Terrorism (Findlaw)
  news.findlaw.com/legalnews/us/terrorism/documents/index.html

- Terrorism Law and Policy (Jurist)
  jurist.law.pitt.edu/terrorism.htm

- Updates on War Against Terrorism (CrimeLynx)
  www.crimelynx.com/terrorism.html

- Vienna Convention on Consular Relations (1963) (Article 36 Communication and Contact With Nationals of the Sending State)
  www.un.org/law/ilc/texts/consul.htm

- West Group Crisis Response Team
  company.findlaw.com/pr/2001/091301.wtc2.html

- World Trade Center Attack: Official Documents (Columbia University Libraries)
  web.columbia.edu/cu/lweb/indiv/dsc/wtc.html

Insider's Guide to Criminal Justice Resources

- World Trade Center Disaster Assistance (NYSBA) www.nysba.org/wtc/index.htm
- World Trade Center Disaster Recovery (NYS Archives and State Historical Records Advisory Board) www.nyshrab.org/WTC/wtc.html

GLOSSARY

ASCII: American Standard Code for Information Interchange is a protocol for substituting numbers for letters of the alphabet and other characters. ASCII files are unadorned text posted on many web sites because they can be read by most programs.

Boolean Logic: The relationships among search terms can be ordered through Boolean connectors, e.g., AND, OR, NOT, to narrow or broaden search results

DSL: Digital Subscriber Line is a service that provides fast access (much faster than a modem) to the Internet through conventional telephone lines.

Hits: Search results or individual pages found through an Internet search engine.

HTML: Hypertext Markup Language is a code used to create documents that can be viewed on the Internet using a web browser.

HTTP: HyperText Transfer Protocol is the means for transferring files and information, particularly web pages, through the Internet. It precedes most web addresses, e.g., http://www.nysda.org.

Hyperlinks and Hypertext: Connections between links on one web page to another web page, document, or another portion of the same web page.

Invisible Web (Deep Web): Web content, such as databases, hidden below the surface of the web and not indexed by conventional search engines. It is the material typically discovered by using a specific web page's search site engine.

Internet: Network of networks linking myriad computers databases worldwide.

ISDN: Integrated Services Digital Network is a method for providing high-speed access to the Internet through phone lines using digital circuitry.

Modem (Dial-up Modem): Hardware used to communicate with an Internet Service Provider or database host by converting signals sent through telephone lines.

PDF: Portable Document Format is a method for posting documents on the web that can be read by using an Adobe Acrobat Reader. The software can be downloaded for free at www.adobe.com and operates seamlessly through your web browser.

Portal: An Internet Portal is a web page that contains access points to search engines, news sources, specialty databases and other pages. They are gaining popularity due to their comprehensiveness and convenience.

RTF: Rich Text Format is an interchange format that allows documents to be read by most programs.

URL (Web Address): Uniform Resource Locator is the address of a web site on the Internet.

Web Browser (Internet Browser): Program for accessing information on the World Wide Web, such as Internet Explorer or Netscape.

WWW: World Wide Web is the part of the Internet in which information is connected through computers using hypertext links.

FURTHER READING

- Bibliography of Internet Books (ABA 2001)
  www.abanet.org/lpm/magazine/booklist.html

- Criminal Justice Research in Libraries and on the Internet (Greenwood Publishing Group 2nd ed. 1997)
  www.greenwood.com/books/BookDetail.asp?dept_id=1&sku=GR0048

- Guide to Immigration and Legal Research on the Internet (AILA rev'd ed. 2000)
  www.ailapubs.org/ailguidtoima.html

- Internet Guide for the Legal Researcher (Infosources Publishing 3rd ed. 2001)
  www.infosourcespub.com/book3.cfm

- Internet Guide for New York Lawyers (NYSBA 1999)
  www.nysba.org/cle/newbookscat/4123/4123.html

- New York Legal Research Guide (William S. Hein 2nd ed. 1998)
  www.wshein.com/catalog/gut.asp?titleno=311220

COMPANION CD-ROM

The companion CD-ROM created for this book contains the complete text of *The Insider's Guide* in PDF format. A copy of the Adobe Acrobat Reader has been included—the newest version can be downloaded from the Adobe Acrobat web site, www.adobe.com. The PDF version of the book will permit you to directly access any web site by clicking on any hyperlink, provided you are already connected to the Internet.

Begin by inserting the CD-ROM into the CD-ROM Drive. The auto run feature will automatically open the file in the Acrobat Reader. If nothing happens, you will need to open the PDF file manually. Access your CD-ROM drive through Windows Explorer. Open the file named InsidersGuide2002.pdf.

As mentioned in the Preface, some web links are problematic. If you have trouble reaching a web site through the PDF, one way around it is to copy and paste the full URL into the address line of your web browser, then press the Enter key. If it still does not work, try to reach the root of the web site to determine if the address of that particular page or document has changed or has been removed. The root is the portion of a web address that typically comes before a slash (e.g., www.nysda.org is the root of http://www.nysda.org/Defense_News/defense_news.html).

The Adobe Acrobat Reader has a Find Command to aid you in searching the book by a specific word or phrase. The Find Command can be found in the Edit menu or on the tool bar as the binocular icon. The Table of Contents are also hyperlinked.

For technical questions or problems related to using the CD-ROM, contact Dave Austin, Director of Information Technology at the New York State Defenders Association, daustin@nysda.org.